Praise for

Make Learning Magi

"Are your students missing that twinkle of curiosity in their eyes? Are you beat down and wondering if your purpose vanished due to the evil spell of educational demands? Throughout the pages of this precious gem, Tisha Richmond vulnerably exposes how her zeal for teaching was disappearing before she began a miraculous, connected journey. She eloquently pens her rediscovery of mystery and wonder to *make learning magical* and wholeheartedly shares strategies and lessons to create a learning atmosphere with the intent to leave a legacy. You find the sparkle to enchant your students with engagement, and after reading this book, the hidden magic that has been buried deep within your soul will burst free and shine brightly for all within your realm of influence. Everything necessary to unlock the magic is right here; you need only to open the pages and begin your journey today."

—**Tara M. Martin**, educator, keynote speaker, and author of *Be REAL*

"*Make Learning Magical* by Tisha Richmond is the book I have been waiting for. The passion, innovation, and love for teaching and inspiring her students is so very evident from the introduction to the final pages. Tisha offers fun and easy-to-implement ideas no matter what subject or grade you teach. I guarantee you will be walking through the wardrobe and into Narnia for many years and lessons to come. Enjoy this book immensely; I sure did!"

—**Adam Welcome**, educator, author of *Run Like a Pirate*, and coauthor of *Kids Deserve It!*

"*Make Learning Magical* combines the value of intentional whimsy, passion, and practical advice to instill the importance of student relationships, learning, ownership, and authenticity. Richmond uses personal and professional stories to show the power that innovative teaching practices can bring to the classroom while weaving in a love for childhood memories and movies. Prepare to feel nostalgia for long ago and inspiration for your students' future as you read *Make Learning Magical*."

—**Mandy Froehlich**, director of innovation and technology, author, speaker, and consultant

"After reading this book, I realize that I have to look for and even expect magic to happen all around me. Tisha shares practical knowledge on how to make your classroom a more fun and inviting environment. She provides touching stories to punctuate her strategies and outlines simple and effective tasks to follow and transform your classroom. This book, with its collection of anecdotes and personal reflections, is one I will be sharing with new and veteran teachers alike. It is full of nuggets of silver, gold, and plenty of weighty glitter—and enough culinary references for another book."

—**Rodney Turner**, virtual educator

"For anyone looking to make a difference and bring about some amazing changes in the classroom, *Make Learning Magical* by Tisha Richmond is the book to read. It is full of inspiration and reminders of the tremendous impact educators have in and out of the classroom, many of which we may never be aware. Tisha's love of learning, growing, and doing what's best for students is evident throughout the entire book. The personal stories from her own experiences as a student and her reflections as an educator remind us of the importance of sharing our stories, being mindful of our 'why,' and continuing to challenge ourselves as educators so we can provide authentic, engaging, and magical learning experiences for our students.

"*Make Learning Magical* offers so many wonderful ideas that can be applied to different content areas and levels, ideas that will draw you in instantly with excitement for creating your own uncommon, student-driven learning experiences in your classroom. The passion that Tisha has for making learning a truly magical experience, not only for her students but for *all* students, is clear throughout the book.

She offers so many unique ideas and practical ways to involve students more in learning—and above all, to promote student voice and student agency in the classroom.

"She guides you step-by-step through the creation of class activities and provides the resources and reassurances needed to get started. The way she shares her own growth process, why she made changes, and her reflections of the impact it has had on her as well as her students are some of the many highlights of this book. Tisha's writing leads you to be more aware of your interactions along with the importance of having kindness and gratitude. She inspires you to take some risks in the classroom that will promote creativity, collaboration, critical thinking, and relationship building.

"She ends each chapter with questions to push your thinking in your own practice and experiences. *Make Learning Magical* is a book full of inspiration about how to make a difference and why it matters. Above all, it's a reminder to focus on relationships and the power of making a connection. Every educator will walk away with ideas for energizing the classroom and creating a welcoming learning space where students design their learning experience and become part of a learning family. Tisha's passion for teaching and learning are clear in this book, which is honest, authentic, and genuinely heartfelt. It will ignite a passion in every educator to be the change, to take a leap, and to *make learning magical*."

—**Rachelle Dene Poth**, foreign language and STEAM teacher, EdTech consultant

"J.K. Rowling says, 'Something magical happens when you read a good book.' From page one, Tisha Richmond brings the reader into her classroom to show us many recipes for how to transform our classrooms into places of whimsy and fun. While I loved reading about her culinary arts students and the various challenges in which Tisha engages her students, I also appreciated her sharing her own personal learning journey. I found myself taking copious notes and forming brainstorming ideas to create my own classroom magic, as Tisha shares so many creative and practical examples and ideas which can easily be applied to any context. This book is a must-read for educators in any role, teaching any subject!"

—**Jennifer Casa-Todd**, teacher/librarian and author of Social LEADia

"Tisha takes us into her journey, connects us to her learning, and shares with us how she infuses them in her teaching. She reminds educators of what they can bring to a classroom and inspires them to create their own magic. Packed full of reflection and lessons, *Make Learning Magical* is the book for educators who are ready to use life's inspiration and their own learning to transform their teaching."

—**Carrie Baughcum**, special education teacher and creator of *Carrie Baughcum: Life. Learning. Doodles . . . Are Heck Awesome!*

"Grab your magic wand and spread joy throughout your classroom with *Make Learning Magical* by Tisha Richmond! Sharing her experiences as a culinary arts teacher, Tisha guides us through innovative learning experiences sprinkled with gamification, intrigue, discovery, and more. Her recipes for success include all the ingredients you need to transform the culture of your classroom, one engaging lesson at a time. You won't need to cast a spell on your students because they will never want to leave! You will find so many great ideas in this book!"

—**Tamara Letter**, technology integrator and instructional coach

"Tisha pulls back the curtain and reveals the secrets of educational 'entertainers' and reminds us that learning is not a show or an illusion. She hits home by showing us that when students are empowered as authentic learners, the magic truly lies within them—and it's the teacher's job to reveal that secret."

—**Jarod Bormann**, author of *Professionally Driven*

MAKE LEARNING *Magical*

Transform Your Teaching and Create *Unforgettable* Experiences in Your Classroom

Tisha Richmond

Make Learning Magical

This book is available at special discounts when purchased in quantity for use as premiums, promotions, fundraisers, or for educational use. For inquiries and details, contact the publisher at books@daveburgessconsulting.com.

Published by Dave Burgess Consulting, Inc.
San Diego, CA
DaveBurgessConsulting.com

Cover Design by Genesis Kohler
Editing and Interior Design by My Writers' Connection

Library of Congress Control Number: 2018956628
Paperback ISBN: 978-1-946444-99-8
Ebook ISBN: 978-1-949595-00-0

First Printing: September 2018

Dedication

To my amazing husband, Russ—
Your love and belief in me has given me wings.

To my incredible children, Ella and Tommy—
You inspire me in countless ways and bring me unspeakable joy.

Contents

What's the Secret Ingredient?

The place I have always seen magic produced is in the kitchen. My mother cooked all the time when I was a child. We were (are) a family of four hungry children and one Italian father who loves food. Every day my mother transformed basic ingredients into wonderful dishes that nourished our bodies as well as our hearts. The truly magical ingredient she imparted into every bite of lasagna and morsel of her Italian beef sandwiches was her love for us. My mother, the best magician there is, taught me the power of cooking with love.

As I got older and started to cook for myself, I began to see the true magic of food. I learned that my mother was building much more than sandwiches; she was building memories through meaningful moments that brought family and friends together. *Make Learning Magical* by Tisha Richmond shows us how to impart this same love into our lessons and, thus, create those magical, classroom moments full of memories lasting well beyond the bell.

As a former culinary arts teacher, Tisha knows all too well the magic that can be created when people come together. While her book shows us many ways to build those moments into our classrooms, the real magic she shares in her stories comes from her relationships with those she serves. Thank you, Tisha, for reminding us that the true secret ingredient is love. Like food, a well-designed lesson, built with care and made with love will transform the world one bite at a time.

Bon appetit!

Michael Matera
Teacher, Speaker, and Youtuber, author of *Explore Like a Pirate*, mrmatera.com

Introduction

Investors are coming!
You have forty minutes to finalize your signature dishes and prepare your presentations before our guests arrive.

My classroom seems to vibrate with excitement as students walk into a culinary world where they are no longer high school students but food truck owners about to complete a very important mission. The warning above lets them know time is of the essence. In less than an hour, they will reveal their delicious creations and present their marketing pitches to a room full of eager investors. As the clock counts down, students greet investors (staff members and local chefs) as they arrive and hand them each a clipboard with an evaluation form (rubrics) and $2,000 in play money. Once all the investors are present, a promo video introduces the food truck teams, and another student explains the instructions: Each team will present its food truck name, logo, and plated signature dish along with a sample for each investor. As the investors taste-test the food, students present their marketing pitches and explain why they chose their signature dish and how they plan to adapt as they travel across the United States.

I stand in the back of the room, my eyes welling with tears as I watch my students shine. They are completely immersed in the moment. They are empowered food truck entrepreneurs pitching their concepts to a room full of investors. This excitement and passion—this *magic*—is what makes learning come alive! It is what I love about teaching. But my classroom wasn't always so magical.

Four years ago, I was going through a rough season in my educational journey. I was stressed and worn out. Comfortable in my teaching practice, I felt stagnant. As the lone culinary teacher in my department, I didn't have anyone nearby to bounce ideas off of. Most days, I just went through the motions. On the worst days, I dreamed of leaving the teaching profession to work as a barista where I would spend hours creating beautiful latte art. When I think back on those dreams now, I wonder what made the idea of being a barista so appealing—*why did I dream of running from teaching into the perceived comfort of the coffee shop?* The answer has to do with joy or, rather, the lack of it. During that time, I felt as if all joy had been stripped from my teaching and replaced with deadlines, initiatives, and requirements. I got so busy jumping through hoops that I lost sight of what was most important: the students.

The good news is I never made the leap to barista. Things began to turn around for me when I received a grant from US Cellular and Carl Perkins to purchase a classroom set of iPads. I knew immediately that I wanted these iPads to be much more than a tool for searching recipes online; I wanted them to transform learning in my classroom. Unsure about how to make that happen, I searched for EdTech conferences where I could learn more about integrating these devices into my teaching practice. Attending that first EdTech conference opened up a whole new world for me. I discovered digital tools and innovative teaching practices and was introduced to the power of Twitter for educators. I felt as if I had walked through the wardrobe and into Narnia! Throughout the event, awe-inspiring educators connected via Twitter handles, shared hashtags, and posted resources from sessions. I had felt alone for so long, and now I realized I had instant access to a magical space of connected learning.

Soon after the conference, I found a contest on Twitter to earn a free registration and hotel for Miami Device, an EdTech conference that just happened to land on my birthday week. To submit an entry, you were required to create something describing why you wanted to attend and then share it with the world through some social media platform. Feeling inspired and courageous by my new learning, I made the move from being a Twitter consumer to a Twitter creator. I created a submission by smashing together a few of the apps I had just learned about: Tellagami, Thinglink, and Paper by 53. I included a note about my new excitement and love for educational technology, and thinking it couldn't hurt, I added that I thought it would be a fabulous way to celebrate my fortieth birthday. With a deep breath and a nervous stomach, I launched my submission into the Twittersphere and waited. To be honest, I didn't think I had any chance of winning, but what did I have to lose other than a little of my pride? I waited and waited and waited some more until finally, I saw the announcement—I had won!

Attending Miami Device marked an important turning point for me. I spent two incredible days learning and establishing amazing relationships. On the last day of the conference, a group of educators gathered and talked about going to South Beach for dinner. I didn't know any of them well, but my other option was to celebrate my fortieth birthday alone in my hotel room. So I went to dinner and ended up finding my tribe. We continue to talk on Voxer, and through those relationships, I've learned and grown and been introduced to many other amazing educators. I came to realize that I don't have to work in a silo—even as an elective teacher. I can learn from educators from around the world who teach in various grade levels and subject areas, and I have ideas to share as well!

It is safe to say that since that November day in 2014, I have grown exponentially as an educator. My joy and passion for education hasn't just been restored; it has been completely transformed. I have never been as excited about teaching and learning as I am now after twenty-one years in education. Through this journey of learning, I have found seven magical components that have contributed to infusing joy and passion into my teaching and transforming my classroom into a place where learning truly comes alive. In the chapters to follow, I will break down these seven components and share with you how I've tapped into their power in my classroom and, better yet, how you can *too.*

But first, let's talk a little about magic.

Chapter 1

Magical Learning

Ask what makes you come alive and go do it. Because what the world needs is people who have come alive.

—Howard Thurman

I have two children, both extremely intelligent but wired differently. My daughter has always played the game of school really well. She understands the rules, and when they change slightly from one teacher to the next, she adapts. My son, on the other hand, has never quite understood the game. He is an out-of-the-box thinker who, instead of learning the rules, wants to make his own. He always seeks to understand the relevance of what he is learning and how it connects to life. I get that because I remember sitting in class listening to the teacher's instructions with all my might. I wanted to understand what was being said but was often unable to connect the pieces. It was common for me to turn to my neighbor after receiving an assignment and ask in embarrassment, "So what are we supposed to do?" In the few classes that had me up and moving, creating, thinking critically, and collaborating, I found ways to make meaningful learning connections. I thrived in those classes. Unfortunately, I didn't have enough of these experiences to find my true passion or to discover joy in learning; in fact, I went through my high school years feeling like I wasn't smart or creative enough to reach for my dreams. I went to college with no idea about what I wanted to do. I hoped that, somehow, I would find my passion along the way. Interestingly enough, it was not knowing that helped me find my true calling.

Some people feel an inexplicable pull toward education. For others, teaching is a childhood dream come true. My story isn't so romantic. Having begun college with an undeclared major, I felt a wave of terror when, at the end of my sophomore year, my college guidance counselor told me, "Tisha, your time is up. You must declare a major."

Although I didn't have a career path mapped out, I knew I wanted to make a difference in the lives of others. I had no clue what that would look like, and quite frankly, I lacked the confidence to believe I could make a meaningful impact. In retrospect, I can see that my own confusion and fear about not knowing what to do with my life served as the catalyst that propelled me toward education; I wanted to help students discover their life's purpose. With that passion as my purpose, I have taught more than 5,040 students in the past twenty-plus years. It brings me such joy to know I have had the opportunity to help so many students discover their passions and become empowered to pursue them. The best moments I have experienced in my career are those when the light in my students' eyes shine—and you can all but see them thinking, *I can learn this. I* ***want*** *to learn this.* And even better, *I want to share this with others!* To me, that's magical.

Don't Miss the Magic

Magical moments are rare in most classes—and in life in general. Or rather, they are rarely noticed. One day during my holiday shopping a few years back, I came across a wall hanging with a Roald Dahl quote that made me pause:

> **"And above all, watch with glittering eyes the whole world around you because the greatest secrets are always hidden in the most unlikely places. Those who don't believe in magic will never find it."**

The words made me think: *How often do I miss the magic in the mundane and busy moments of life? Do I truly watch the world around me with glittering eyes, or am I too hurried, consumed, and pre-occupied to notice?*

From that moment, I tried to be intentional about enjoying the slower pace of what was left of the winter break. I determined to view the world through glittering eyes and experience the magic of life. Just a few days later, the girls in my family went to a local musical production of *Mary Poppins.* As the stage came to life with singing, dancing, beautiful costumes, and special effects, I watched my six-year-old niece's eyes glitter with wonder. She was completely mesmerized by every scene.

I could relate because I felt the same excitement and wonder the first time I watched *Mary Poppins* at the movie theater as a child. It quickly became my favorite movie. I listened to the soundtrack on a record over and over again until I had memorized the words to every song. I can still remember hanging upside down on our backyard jungle gym repeating the word "*Supercalifragilisticexpialidocious*" until I was able to speak it fluidly. But I didn't stop there. Once I had mastered learning how to say that fantastical word, I learned how to say it backwards. The magic of *Mary Poppins* captivated me; I wanted to bring that magic into my own life by learning everything I could about it.

That is how I want my students to feel about learning in my classroom. I want their eyes to glitter with anticipation and wonder. I want them to go home and take the learning further by practicing the cooking methods and adding their own special twists and creative touches. I always hope they will share their learning with others by serving their creations to their family and friends. The goal is to do far more than create one-off experiences. Each magical learning moment will lead to another. If you watch for magic, it can become an everyday occurrence.

A Spoonful of Sugar

Mary Poppins knew how to make even the most mundane tasks fun and memorable. When she sang "A Spoonful of Sugar," the chore of cleaning turned into a game, which makes me think, *Why do we so often treat learning like a chore? What if we approached learning itself as fun—as something to be undertaken in wonder, curiosity, and play?*

My childhood hero, Fred Rogers, said, "Play is often talked about as if it were a relief from serious learning. But for children, play is serious learning. Play is really the work of childhood." I have found this statement to be absolutely true in my teaching experience and have worked hard to create a classroom environment that makes exploration and play integral in the classroom. The truth is that no matter what topic, when we are doing something we enjoy, the learning becomes meaningful; we make associations with the learning that are rich and memorable.

Play and fun are not synonymous with simple and easy. There is an abundance of challenge, strategy, and deep thinking associated with play. My six-year-old niece has a wild imagination. I'm always astonished by the stories she conjures up when we play together. We'll often enter a make-believe world where our surroundings come to life (not unlike the world of *Mary Poppins)*. The impressive degree of creativity she uses to develop this world and the vocabulary she engages in are almost always related to things she's recently experienced or learned at school. Playing make-believe is her way of demonstrating her understanding of the world around her. Board games reveal another aspect of play. Each move she makes shows the strategy and deep thinking she is experiencing. She is immersed fully and thinking about what she needs to do to win!

When students learn through play, it changes their perspective from one of compliance to one of wonder and curiosity. It allows them to delve deeper into the content, ask questions, and think more critically about what they are learning than if I simply feed them information to memorize. When students experience learning this way, they are truly able to tap into the joy of learning and discover their passions. Creating a classroom that is playful is all about mindset and how *you* approach learning. If you get excited and show enthusiasm for what you are teaching, your enjoyment will be contagious. Students will catch it, and their mindset toward learning will change, too, from a chore to one of curiosity. Making this move toward play doesn't necessarily mean completely uprooting all of the teaching practices you've honed over the years. Start thinking about your course content in a playful way, and just as Mary Poppins suggests, "find the fun, and snap! The job's a game!"

Laughter Is the Best Medicine

One of the most enjoyable side effects of play is laughter. You've heard the saying, "Laughter is the best medicine." I completely agree. I can immediately think of the people in my life who are "contagious laughers." They find the funny in most any situation, and their laughter is so contagious that soon, everyone around them is laughing too.

My mom is one of my favorite contagious laughers. Her ability to find the humor in life makes her fun to be around. She is the best person to watch a comedy with because her laugh is so genuine and boisterous that the whole room rolls laughing right along with her.

In *Mary Poppins*, Bert, played by Dick Van Dyke, is a "contagious laugher." Bert is a kite salesman, chimney sweep, one-man band, and sidewalk chalk artist, and he finds joy in each job. A song that demonstrates his joy beautifully is "I Love to Laugh" that he sings with Uncle Albert, who suffers from a serious condition that is triggered by laughing. When he gets going, he can't stop, and that uncontrollable laughter causes him to float to the ceiling. As Bert, Mary Poppins, and the children arrive to help Uncle Albert off the ceiling, Bert says, "Whatever you do, keep a straight face. Last time it took us three days to get him down." Of course the more they all try to keep a straight face, the more they laugh, and before long, they're all floating and singing about how much they love to laugh.

Laughter, like smiling, is contagious. When we are around laughter, it's difficult not to join in. Someone begins to giggle, and before long, others do too. And that's a good thing! In a *Forbes* magazine article titled "Six Science-Based Reasons Why Laughter Is the Best Medicine," the writer refers to laughter as a "potent drug with the contagious power of a virus that conveys a slew of benefits for the mind and body." Among the benefits listed are . . .

- Laughter is a potent endorphin releaser.
- Laughter contagiously forms social bonds.
- Laughter fosters brain connectivity.
- Laughter is central to relationships.
- Laughter has an effect similar to antidepressants.
- Laughter protects your heart.

Wow! Those are some pretty powerful benefits! I want to be more like Bert and Uncle Albert, fostering a classroom so full of joy from contagious laughter and learning that I can't get my students down from the ceiling. I want to create learning opportunities that foster laughter . . .

More play,
More games,
More challenges,
More creativity,
More wonder,
More collaboration,
More silliness.

Because laughter, like play—like magic—makes learning stick. Joy-filled moments make learning meaningful. They help students make connections to the material in ways that stodgy, traditional teaching approaches simply can't.

Create Magical Experiences

We can be intentional about creating magical experiences for our students just as the amazing cast of *Mary Poppins* did. Magic is all around us if we truly look for it; it's all about perspective. Stop for a moment and consider where you may be missing out on magic: Do you hurry through life focusing on to-dos, missed opportunities, and failures or regrets? Does stress or a constant awareness of lack of time nag at your thoughts? Or do you choose to look with glittering eyes at the magic that surrounds you?

We can learn so much from the daily interactions with those we encounter and life's everyday happenings when we choose to. As you seek to make learning magical in your classroom, use your imagination and make play and wonder part of your students' classroom experience.

- ✴ What props or decorations could you use to make your classroom fun and even fanciful? Check out the dollar store (or your attic or garage) for low-priced and free ideas.
- ✴ When you take a walk, be intentional about noticing the beauty of your surroundings. How could you bring your students outdoors to experience it—or how you could bring nature inside?
- ✴ When you watch television, watch for themes from your students' favorite shows that you can layer over your curriculum to make your content come to life.
- ✴ Get to know the owners and staff of local businesses. Whom could you invite into your classroom as guest experts?
- ✴ Do you worry that laughter will get "out of hand" in the classroom and detract from learning? How might you use laughter and play to *enhance* learning in your classroom?

How many great secrets do we miss by not paying attention? How many missed opportunities have passed us by? In *Mary Poppins*, Bert sensed that something was brewing and about to begin. He understood that the greatest treasures are hidden in the most unlikely places. Aware of the world of possibilities around him, he watched for the magic of life with glittering eyes.

The first step toward making learning magical for your students is to believe in magic.

Chapter 2
Memorable Beginnings

As I wearily approached the hotel's front desk after a long day of traveling, the desk clerk greeted me with an infectious smile and a warm welcome. He immediately asked how my day had been—a question you'd expect from someone in the hospitality industry. But it was his genuine manner that surprised me. His smile wasn't forced, and his greeting felt real. Then he surprised me again when, with a flick of the wrist, he revealed a fanned out hand of playing cards and enthusiastically asked, "Would you like to see some magic?" Did this guy know whom he was talking to?

"Heck, yes, I'm ready for some magic!" I replied. Immediately, a burst of energy replaced my fatigue as this kind man performed his card trick with skillful sleight of hand, magically revealing the card I had secretly chosen from the deck. Wow! I was amazed! After the magic trick, he asked if there was anything else I needed to make my stay more comfortable, and he had me on my way with my key and Wi-Fi password. Within minutes, I had gone from exhausted to energized all because of someone's hospitality and passion for his work. It was what I call a magical beginning, and it all started with a little hospitality.

The Magic of Hospitality

Hospitality is defined as "the friendly and generous reception and entertainment of guests, visitors, or strangers." In the book *Setting the Table*, author Danny Meyer states, "Virtually nothing else is as important as how one is made to feel in any business transaction. Hospitality exists when you believe the other person is on your side." In this business transaction, I definitely was made to feel like the desk clerk was on my side. He was skillful at making me feel a range of emotions within a very short time: laughter, curiosity, comfort, excitement, and joy. I left the front desk knowing that he was on my side; he would ensure that my stay was enjoyable. Now *that* is hospitality at its finest!

As I reflected on the hospitality I received during my stay at that hotel, I considered the importance of hospitality in our schools. How do our students feel when they enter our schools and classroom? Do they believe we are on their sides? How different would our schools be if students were all greeted with as warm and memorable of a welcome as I received checking into a hotel?

The following three elements characterize the hospitality I encountered during my hotel stay. Let's look at each and think about how it could translate to our classrooms:

A Warm Welcome

The desk clerk greeted me with a smile and a genuine "How are you?" I felt as if he truly wanted to know how my day had been. Our students recognize the authenticity (or lack of it) of our interactions with them. They can see through a fake smile and a forced "How are you?" How are we greeting our students when they come into our classrooms? Are we welcoming students with excited and genuine smiles, or are we preoccupied with other tasks?

An Entertaining Hook

After making me feel welcomed, the desk clerk surprised me by revealing a handful of cards and asking if I wanted to see a magic trick. It was unexpected, and I was immediately intrigued and excited to participate. In *Teach Like a Pirate*, author Dave Burgess shares multiple presentation strategies designed to hook students and draw them into your lesson. This guy had his presentation strategy down! I was hooked! What hooks could you use in your lesson to engage students and get them fired up about learning?

Passion and Enthusiasm

Not only was I hooked by his entertaining magic trick, but his enthusiasm and passion captivated me! The desk clerk tapped into something he was passionate about and brought it into his work. Dave Burgess writes, "Bringing your personal passion to the classroom empowers you to create a more powerful lesson because you are teaching from an area of strength." Magic was definitely one of this guy's strengths! By bringing something he was passionate about into his everyday interactions, he was empowered to create a powerful experience for me. Is there something you are passionate about that you could incorporate into the classroom to bring excitement and a powerful experience for your students?

Creating a Hospitable Environment

Students deserve our finest service. From the moment they walk into our classrooms, they should feel welcomed and as if we are on their sides. As the famous saying goes, "You never get a second chance to make a first impression." First impressions are powerful, and that is no different in the classroom; the tone is set the moment our students set foot in our doors. We feel hospitality with all of our senses: the look, feel, sounds, and smells all add to the overall atmosphere and experience. Those factors draw students in—or make them want to walk away. I know that my classroom is quite possibly the only home some of my students have, so making it a place where they feel welcomed, nurtured, and safe is my primary concern—when students' basic needs are not met, learning will not take place. Here are a few ways I work to make my classroom a place that feels inviting:

Decor

I've enjoyed arranging furniture and designing interior spaces for as long as I can remember. My family still teases me about the mint green and peach with which I painted my room in high school. I think that I even painted my door knobs peach! A fun weekend would involve rearranging my furniture in new and visually appealing ways to make the most efficient use of space. Though my color scheme has become much more subtle as I've aged, and my furniture doesn't get shuffled around nearly as much, I still love playing with color schemes and furniture arrangements.

During my first three years at my current high school, I had the opportunity to teach a section of interior design. I loved teaching that class and seeing the creativity that my students demonstrated in designing their floor plans and color schemes. One of the units I taught was on the psychology of color. We may not pay particular attention to the color schemes of our surroundings, but they can greatly affect how we feel without us realizing it; for example, blue isn't often used in restaurants because it suppresses people's appetites, but it is used in many other spaces such as doctor's offices because of its calming effect. Red is energy producing and is known to increase heart rate. Understanding some of the emotions that colors produce can help us create an atmosphere that is conducive to learning and foster the feelings we want students to have in our classrooms. Here is a breakdown of the emotions associated with some popular colors:

Red: This invigorating color can have a positive effect on memory and can help students focus if used in small doses. Too much of this stimulating and exciting color can have a negative effect, causing stress, frustration, and anger.

Orange: This vibrant color has been known to be a mood lifter, promoting feelings of comfort and welcome. Improving neural functioning and increasing oxygen to the brain, orange stimulates mental activity, boosts energy, improves focus, and promotes increased productivity and organization. Due to the energy and brightness this color produces, too much of it can be overstimulating to the young or kids with oodles of energy. Like red, this color is best in small doses. It's good for highlighting important facts and information and used with intention during specific types of learning activities.

Yellow: There is a reason why the iconic "happy face" emoji is yellow. This color helps to release a chemical in the brain called serotonin that produces feelings of happiness. Yellow enhances concentration by giving the nervous system and brain a wakeup call. As with most everything, there can be too much of a good thing. Heavy doses of yellow can be difficult on the eye and cause fatigue.

Green: Restfulness and calm are feelings associated with this soothing color. Found readily in nature, green is soothing to the eyes and helps relax the body and alleviate stress. This color is also restorative, helping to boost mental resources that can revitalize learning. It is also known to promote efficiency and focus as well as long-term concentration and clarity.

Blue: This relaxing color has a soothing effect, producing calming chemicals in the brain. Combined with the positive benefits of improving reading comprehension, enhancing creativity, and promoting high levels of thought and productivity, blue is a great color to integrate into the learning environment. Lighter shades have a friendly effect, while darker shades tend to be more somber.

Pink: The most tranquil of all colors, known to reduce feelings of anxiety and anger.

Purple: This color helps promote deep thought and is associated with creativity, mystery, and *magic*! Using purple in learning experiences where you are encouraging curiosity, wonder, and mystery could be a powerful way to use this color.

The colors you use to decorate your room can have a positive or negative effect on the learning environment. The color you use in your space can be a powerful factor in creating an environment that promotes positive emotions and learning. Even something as simple as picking a background or font color in a slide presentation, learning activity, or game can make a difference in the emotional response of your students. Color choice may not be something we immediately think of when designing our bulletin boards or putting up posters, but everything in your room, from colors to textures, can affect the way your students feel and learn in your classroom.

Due to the nature of my subject area, my class is broken into two spaces. Half of the room is for demonstrations and instruction, and the other half is broken into eight kitchens. In the instruction part of the room, I tend to use soothing greens and blues in larger amounts on my bulletin boards with little pops of pink for added tranquility, orange to lift moods and stimulate mental abilities, and joyful yellow to increase overall happiness. In the kitchen area, I have each station labeled by color: red, orange, yellow, green, blue, purple, pink, and silver. This is partly because it's an easy way to label and identify kitchen equipment, but it also produces a whimsical element to the room. In the book, *Colors for Your Every Mood*, author Leatrice Eiseman describes spaces decorated with whimsical colors as "lighthearted, playful, capricious and alive." She refers to them as jelly bean colors that are found where joy prevails and that will make you happier than any other colors. I never intentionally chose my kitchen colors for this reason, but looking back, those are emotions that I definitely associate with my learning space.

Similar to the effect of color on emotions, our physical arrangement of our space can have an effect as well. Clutter can create a sense of chaos, while tranquil and organized spaces can make you and your students feel calm. I am in my classroom for more hours a day than I am in my own home, so creating a space that feels "homey" is important for me as well as for my students. I love creating a space that fits my own unique personality and style. If I'm comfortable in my space, I hope that my students will be too. I try to keep things as clutter free as possible, so all materials are easy to locate when needed. Is this always the case? Absolutely not. My class definitely has messy days, but I try to maintain a sense of organization so my students feel comfortable and free from chaos.

Coffee Bar

Confession: I have a little bit of a coffee addiction. Maybe it's because I live in the Pacific Northwest, and we've had a coffee drive-through on every corner since long before Starbucks came up with the idea. I love a good cup of coffee. To feed my coffee addiction, and more importantly to create a warm, inviting space, I've set up a coffee bar in the back of my classroom. It's complete with a Keurig maker, hot water kettle, mugs, teas, assorted K-Cups, and Torani Syrups. Students can earn a Chance Card for demonstrating extraordinary employability skills or winning special challenges. They choose the cards at random, and some of them are redeemable for a trip to the coffee bar. When redeemed, students get one K-cup to use to prepare a beverage of choice during class. Students love the opportunity to visit the coffee bar and choose their favorite mug and hot beverage. It's amazing how the addition of this space immediately made it feel more welcoming and "homey."

Music

Just as the look of our surroundings affect us, sounds play a role in how we feel in a space. The addition of music changes the tone of a room instantaneously. I use music to help create the mood that I want to set. If students are going to be stepping into a challenge, I play dramatic adventure music. If it is an average day of cooking, I may play Jack Johnson or Imagine Dragons. I also have opportunities for students to stream their music. One of the Chance Cards students can draw is called "Let the Music Play." When they redeem this card, they can take over Pandora for the day and choose the music for the class (as long as it's appropriate). Students love to have a little agency over the music in the classroom, and I love allowing them to show a little of their personality.

Aroma

The aromas that come from my culinary classroom are much different than those that waft through most other spaces in the school. Some days those smells are good, and some days we are opening all the windows and doors and turning on the fans.

I realize that some districts have policies that prevent the use of aroma plugins or appliances, but if you are able to fill your room with pleasing scents, it can definitely help make the room inviting.

You

Though all of the above factors can play a big role in creating a welcoming environment for all who enter, the most important factor in creating a hospitable and welcoming atmosphere is you. The way you greet your students as they walk into the room makes an enormous impact. It is easy to get hurried and distracted by all of the urgent needs that are bombarding us from all directions, but taking the time to be present and welcoming as they enter can be what turns a child's day around.

It's important to remember that our classrooms are a refuge for many students. Some can't wait to walk through our doors. When we greet them with a smile, handshake, and hello, it's like they are coming home. Not too long ago, a student walked into my room and said something that echoed in my mind for the rest of day: "Mrs. Richmond, I think you're the only teacher I have that is actually excited to see me walk into the room." This kid can be a handful, and I could only imagine the havoc he was capable of causing. To be completely honest, there were days I was not excited to see him walk through my door, but I would never let him know that; instead, I tried to put myself in his shoes. I knew his home life was tumultuous at best. Thinking about the chaos that filled his world helped me to empathize and think about how I could make his world just a bit better. For sixty-eight minutes a day, my classroom could be a home he'd never had.

Think about how it feels to walk into a room where people are excited to see you, and you are welcomed with a smile. There have been events that I have dreaded going to, but when I walked in and was welcomed by name with a huge smile, handshake, or hug, I immediately felt as if I belonged. We all long to have a place in this world to feel we belong. As teachers we have an opportunity each day to be that place for our kids, and it starts the moment they walk through our doors.

The Power of a Name

As a little girl, I would rotate turnstile displays of personalized items—bracelets, barrettes, necklaces—looking through the Ts in hopes of finding one with the name "Tisha" on it. I never did. As an adult, I find myself going to those turnstiles again, just as I did as a little girl, looking for my name. The variety of names today is more diverse than it once was, and I light up when I see my name. Not too long ago, I found my name on a bottle of Coke. I could hardly believe it! Of course I bought it because I knew that I may never come across my name on a bottle of Coke again.

Seeing your name on a bottle of Coke or a bracelet or hearing it said by someone who knows and loves you just feels good. It doesn't matter if your name is unique or common; everyone wants to be known *by name*.

During the first few weeks of the semester, I intentionally learn the names of my students. As students participate in activities, I go around the room one by one trying to memorize names. My students' expressions as I try to memorize their names tell me they don't believe I really will be able to do it. Those doubtful glances quickly turn to interest, however, as I start recalling names one by one.

This simple act of name memorization is one of the most powerful things you can do at the start of the semester. Taking the time to show you care enough to know your students by name makes a lasting impact. Don't ever underestimate the power of a name.

Favorite Things

Another one of my all-time favorite movies is *The Sound of Music.* I especially love the scene when all of the Von Trapp children come running into Maria's room during a thunderstorm in search of comfort and safety. She quickly shifts their attention away from the thunderstorm and fears by breaking out into a song about a few of her favorite things. By directing their focus toward things all of them love, happiness replaces fear. The same thing can happen in our classrooms.

When I read *Teach Like a Pirate* by Dave Burgess, I realized I needed to rethink the first days of school. Instead of diving into syllabi and procedures, why not first dive into the things that we are most passionate about and take time to establish a positive environment where students feel safe and supported? Making that shift created a meaningful beginning that has profoundly changed the way I connect with new students. Instead of overwhelming them with information, I focus on getting to know them individually by learning about their favorite things. Inspired by Dave Burgess's playdough activity, let me share with you how my first two days of class unfold:

As students walk in, *The Sound of Music*'s "Favorite Things" song plays in the background. On the screen are instructions to sit down anywhere they would like and write their three favorite things on their stainless steel tables with dry erase markers. When they are done, they talk about their favorite things with the person sitting next to them. Once everyone is seated, I share a slideshow of my favorite things—my passions. Then I ask them to do something that high school students don't expect. I open three large tubs of freshly made, brightly colored "playdough" and tell them to sculpt one of their favorite things. They can choose as much or little dough as they want with any variety of colors. They are free to spread out and find a comfortable place to craft their creation. As students work on their sculptures, I walk around and engage in conversations about what they are making. It doesn't take long for everyone to get immersed in their work and engaged in discussions about their favorite things. My simple questions often lead to more involved descriptions that reveal a lot about them. Some students share personal tidbits, while others stick to surface-level conversations, but they all enjoy the process. Lots of laughter and chatter ensue as classmates share about themselves in a non-threatening and fun way. I have them write their name next to their creations, and I take a picture so I can remember and use them as conversation starters in the weeks to come as I get to know them better.

On the second day of class, I take the favorite things to the next level. I measure out enough ingredients for eight teams to make Rice Krispy Treats. Epic adventure music plays this time as students enter the room and line up by their birthdates down the center of the room—January on one end, December on the other. I count off from Red through Silver (my kitchen colors) until all students have a place to go. Then everyone goes to their kitchens, and I reveal the Rice Krispy Challenge: They will be making Rice Krispy treats with a twist. Instead of the traditionally square Rice Krispy Treats, they will be shaping their treats into something that all the team members share in common. It can be a combination of each team member's favorite things or something entirely different that they discover they have in common. They are also free to mix in any of the specialty ingredients I provide—candy eyes, spray glitter, sprinkles, food coloring, etc.—to show their creativity and add artistic flare. In the process, students get to know their classmates and share what they love. While students collaborate on their creations, I circulate the room, encouraging dialogue as I learn their names. When the creations are complete, I take a picture and mirror them to my Apple TV. After students finish cleaning up, we gather, and each team introduces themselves and explains their creation. This allows us to hear everyone's names and learn something new about each of our classmates. Use LEGO bricks for a variation to this activity. Dump a pile in the middle of the table and have your students make a LEGO creation out of the team's favorite things.

Our favorite things say a lot about who we are and what we are passionate about. They can hold memories or connections to special people in our lives or reveal our dreams and the things we hold close to our hearts. It's amazing how taking a few days at the beginning of the semester to focus on passions and relationship building completely changes the tone and feel of the class. When students are given an opportunity to tap into their passions and share in a non-threatening way, they feel more relaxed and comfortable to talk and get to know one another. And I love the laughter, silliness, and conversations that ensue. Student's personalities begin emerging much sooner than they would otherwise, and the level of enthusiasm and excitement for what's to come is tangible. Syllabi and rules can wait; relationships come first.

Playdough

1 cup flour

½ cup salt

1 cup water

2 T oil

2 T cream of tartar

Food coloring

- Mix first 5 ingredients together in a saucepan and cook on stove over low heat for 3 minutes or until thickened.
- Divide dough into separate portions, add food coloring, and stir.

The Family Table

I'd like to say that, as a culinary teacher, I prepare gourmet dinners every night for my family. The truth is that when I get home, many days, cooking is the last thing I want to do. I've been in a kitchen all day, and to be honest, I'd rather someone else prepare the dinners for me. All that being said, sitting around the dinner table for a family meal is very important to me even when that table is laden with take-out rather than my own home cooking. Something magical happens when we break bread with the people that are important to us. This is where we share the highs and lows of our days, our failures and our successes. This is where we are able to be our true selves, where we feel safe and loved. Over the years, the dinner table has been where my favorite memories and conversations have happened. The table has stains from mugs without coasters and scratches from aggressive game play, but it's where our family bonding has happened.

The sad reality is, many of my students haven't ever felt what it was like to sit around a family table where they felt safe and loved; in fact, my classroom may be the only place they enter in a day where they feel accepted and valued. It is my mission as a teacher to replicate the family table experience in the classroom. I want students to walk into my class feeling safe and loved and bonded with their peers as well as myself. I have days throughout the year where I literally create a family table experience. I have stainless steel tables that are on wheels that get all pushed together into a big square. Students prepare food, and we gather around the "family table" and eat together. There is something special about our family time. There are stories, laughter, and lots of magical memories that are made that bond us together.

The Draft

Team building is a huge part of how I begin the school year. My culinary classes are team oriented, so establishing trust and community right from the get-go is critical. Choosing teams has always been a tricky thing in my lab-based class. Do you let students choose, do you choose for them, or do you randomly select kids? Over the years, I've tried every which way I could to make a list of pros and cons of each method. The past few years, I decided to change it up a bit. As I restructured my first few weeks of instruction to incorporate more relationship and team building activities, I decided I would create a way to make the selection of teams more poignant and meaningful by hosting two weeks of Culinary Boot Camp.

The Culinary Boot Camp includes daily team building challenges that focus on employability skills, such as communication, teamwork, resilience, critical thinking, etc. as well as essential kitchen skills. Because my culinary classes are mixed grade levels, sometimes students know very few people in the room. Creating multiple opportunities to mix and get to know one another is important for creating a safe environment for everyone to learn. Each day we switch groups so that by the end of the two week period, students have worked with nearly everyone. This little push out of their comfort zones at the beginning of the course pays dividends in the long run. By the time we settle into teams after the second week, students aren't nearly as fearful about which team they settle into for the semester.

To make things a bit more exciting, each team challenge provides an opportunity to earn a Mystery Badge. The badge is the size of a baseball card and laminated with a scratch off sticker covering a mystery amount of experience points. Each member of the team that wins the daily challenge collects a Mystery Badge. Students hold onto their badges until the end of the Culinary Boot Camp when all the badges can be scratched off at once to reveal the experience points (XP) they hold. This adds an extra bit of intrigue, as no one knows who is leading because there were differing point values under each one!

The suspense builds throughout the boot camp until the day of "The MasterChef Draft." I adapted this idea from a fantasy-football-style draft pick idea shared with me by *Explore Like a Pirate* author, Michael Matera. This is how it works:

A couple days prior to the draft, I have each student fill out a MasterChef resume on a Google Form. On this resume, they include their name, class period, three strengths, three areas of growth, and an explanation of why they would be a good team member. Using a Google extension called "Save to Doc," I print the resumes on individual sheets of paper and give each student a number that I write on the bottom of each resume and on a class roster. Once they are all numbered, I cut off the names so only the period number, strengths, growth areas, and explanation are visible.

Then it is time for the draft! Students come in to the sound of dramatic music playing and a message on the screen to get out their Mystery Experience Points and scratch them off to reveal the amounts. An immediate buzz of excitement fills the room as students reveal their points. I walk around collecting XP and writing down how much each student earned on my class roster. It takes me just a few minutes to determine my top eight XP holders. When there is a tie, I bring out my foam dice and have a roll off.

The top eight XP holders become the draft leaders. While all the other students go to the class kitchens to prep for an upcoming recipe, the eight leaders and I begin the draft. I lay all of the resumes out in a grid in the center of the room on two pushed-together tables and have the team leaders gather around to read them. I explain that in order to form a balanced team, they need to think about which resumes would best compliment one another. Before they begin making their selections, I allow them to choose one classmate whom they want on their team who would be a known. I have them write it on an index card, and I slip those resumes off of the grid since they are out of play. Then starting with the top XP holder, each team leader chooses one resume from the grid. As they make their selections, I take the resumes and match them to the numbers on my roster and let them know whom they have chosen. Once all of the team leaders have made their first selection, we go back to the top XP holder again and repeat the process until all students have been selected.

I let them know that in the following class period, students will be cooking with their new teams. The ingredients that they had just measured out will be used by the team assigned to that kitchen the next day to make Cheddar Biscuits—their first cooking lab assignment with their new teams.

The final activity of the period is playing team Kahoot! Students quickly bond as they work together to play a game that draws on all of the learning from the past two weeks. The excitement in the room is palpable—a positive sign of the fun-filled semester of learning to come.

To be honest, I was a little apprehensive when I tried this new approach to team building, but I couldn't be happier with the results. My heart is always touched by how quickly teams start to gel. Starting with the Culinary Boot Camp generated a significant increase in energy, excitement, and overall class camaraderie. Students bond and are pumped to launch into the MasterChef-themed semester! It is the perfect way to build excitement and establish a community right from the start, making for a truly *magical* beginning!

Create Memorable Beginnings

The way your students feel when they come into your classroom impacts the way they learn. This is true every day, but in those first few days of the school year or semester, you are setting the tone for every day that follows. Make the most of beginnings by making them memorable.

- ✳ What vibe does your room have? How do the colors, décor, music, and even smell affect you and your students?
- ✳ Do you know the name of each student in your class? Make it a point to learn each one's name within the first week of class.
- ✳ How could you encourage your students to share their passions—their favorite things?
- ✳ What kinds of activities could you do in your classroom to build a spirit of community and belonging?

You have the power to inspire a love for learning in those you serve. The environment you create and the way you make your students feel all contribute to magical learning experiences.

Chapter 3

Authenticity and Agency

You are unrepeatable. There is a magic about you that is all your own.

—D.M. Dellinger

One of my favorite holiday traditions is decorating our family Christmas tree. I love hauling our ornament boxes from the garage, cranking up the Christmas carols and the fireplace, and gathering in our living room to adorn the tree with memories. Some of my friends have beautifully themed Christmas trees with complementary color combinations. There's no denying that those trees are gorgeous; however, nothing is more beautiful to me than our Christmas tree decorated by ornaments our family has collected through the years. As we hang each one on the tree, we share our memories. We giggle at the wooden skier that has been missing her ski for as long as we can remember. The hand-painted ornaments our kids made with love throughout their elementary years symbolize a special memory and season in our lives. They all have a story to tell. Although some have stood the test of time and others are showing signs of their age, when hung together on the tree, they all glisten as part of a beautiful display; in fact, the broken, lackluster ornaments are among our favorites because they hold special moments that we treasure.

As I think about our eclectic family Christmas tree, I reflect on the individuals who enter our school each day. Like ornaments, some sparkle and glisten while others have been scuffed or even broken by the harshness of life. Each one, however, has a unique story to tell. Without a personal connection, we may not see the beauty from the outside and may be tempted to only display the ones that sparkle. But when we take time to listen and get to know those we serve, we begin to see the light that radiates from within. We can see beyond the brokenness and find their beauty. That's when we are able to recognize their fears and challenges and help them discover their dreams and pursue their passions.

When we help all students understand the important part they play, not only in our school culture but our world, we empower them to radiate with authentic beauty that can shine brightly for all to see. Part of making learning magical is providing the environment and opportunities for our students to find their inner beauty and share it with others. In a world that's often harsh and demanding, many of our students and coworkers are hurting. What they need to *feel* is that they are loved and appreciated for who they are. They need to know they are not alone and that their voice matters. There are so many ways we can empower students to tap into what makes them special and to use their gifts to benefit others. In this chapter, we'll look at how traits of gratitude, kindness, authenticity, and courage can help make learning magical.

The Magic Attitude

What's the magic word? I can't count the number of times my parents and teachers reminded me to say, "please." And just as often, they encouraged me to say, "thank you" to show appreciation when I was growing up. Over time those words became part of my everyday speech, and even now they seem quite magical. When you hear them in everyday interactions, it's like a little sprinkle of pixie dust because saying these words is more than a habit; it's a mindset, an attitude of gratitude. How different would our interactions with people be if everyone had an "attitude of gratitude"—if we perceived our everyday circumstances and interactions as gifts rather than something to which we are entitled?

We have an opportunity to bring an attitude of gratitude into our schools each day. How we react when someone opens a door for us, gives us a compliment, or brings us our mail from the workroom makes such a difference. All of those interactions are an act of kindness, and when we recognize them by showing appreciation and gratitude, we sprinkle a little pixie dust each time.

My husband and I work across the courtyard from each other. He teaches ceramics and I teach culinary arts, two of the messiest classrooms of the whole school to clean. Our custodian is amazing. He comes into my classroom every day with a smile and an enthusiastic greeting. He takes such incredible pride in his work and meticulously cleans our rooms until they sparkle. One day I noticed that he came into my room without his usual smile and had lost the spring in his step. When I asked what was wrong, he told me someone had criticized his work. He went on to say that, in his many years of custodial work, this was only the second complaint he had ever received. He was deflated. All the years he had gone without complaints didn't make up for the fact that someone was unhappy. He felt unappreciated. As I thought about that, I wondered how often he gets compliments for the work he does. His work is often done while others aren't looking. How often had I taken for granted the special details that he prides himself in? Do I really take time to notice when he waxes my floor or washes my windows? How often do we take for granted those people that make our lives easier and more beautiful?

#GratitudeSnaps

Recognizing and then sharing our genuine gratitude for others does two things: It makes the person we're thanking *feel* appreciated, and it helps us remember that so much of life is a gift. Sometimes we need to jump-start an attitude of gratitude, particularly when life isn't going as planned. This past year, my dear friend Tara Martin and I began a movement called #GratitudeSnaps for exactly that reason.

Tara had experienced a difficult week. One negative thought had led to another, and before she knew it, feelings of inadequacy, frustration, and worthlessness consumed her. As she shared her story with me, I could completely relate. I'd been knocked into that pit and had climbed out more than a few times! I said, "We all find ourselves in that place of negativity at times. I know I do! Life is hard and full of unexpected twists, turns, and bumps along the way. You know, when I find myself in that deep, dark place, it always helps to look back at all of the pivotal events that have helped to shape and bring me to where I'm at today. Sometimes those events are positive, and sometimes they are negative. Regardless, they've added to my story and, if nothing else, made me stronger. Girl, look around you; reflect on the positive that is happening in your life—so many amazing things! Reflecting on those times allows me to shift my focus from the negative of my current circumstance to all that I have to be grateful for."

That is when an idea popped into my head: "Hey, Tara! What if you kept a thirty-day gratitude journal? Each day you could write about one thing to be grateful for to help climb out of this negativity pit!" Then another idea hit me upside the head that perfectly fit my dear soul sister, the creator of #BookSnaps: "What about creating

#GratitudeSnaps? Instead of a journal, you could take a daily pic of something you are grateful for, make a snap out of it, then share it out via social media! This would allow you to do what you love: 'create digitally' *and* focus on the positives in your life! Just as #BookSnaps help us connect and draw meaning from the text, #GratitudeSnaps could help connect with the positive that is in our lives in a meaningful way."

Tara loved the idea and took it a step further. She said, "How about we launch a thirty-day #GratitudeSnaps challenge on Twitter to spread positivity and focus on the things we are grateful for?"

Yes!

We decided that the challenge would be to share #GratitudeSnaps of something—a person, thing, or feeling—every day for thirty days. Just like #BookSnaps, people could take pictures with their phone and upload it to SnapChat or another picture app. Within the app, they could add bitmojis, text, and images that connected to what they were grateful for. Then people would use the hashtag #GratitudeSnaps when posting on Twitter to share their attitude of gratitude with the world.

Within weeks, we launched our first #GratitudeSnaps Challenge, and I was blown away with the response from the Twitter community. All that joy and thankfulness was just what our souls needed. Scrolling through the hashtag each day filled my heart with such joy. I saw pictures from educators and students around the globe who were sharing the things that they were most grateful for. The authenticity, love, and emotion reminded me that we are all in this thing called life together. We are not just educators; we are moms, dads, sons, daughters, spouses, grandparents, aunts, uncles, and friends. We are people fueled by passions and dreams and given our own unique set of circumstances. Life can be full of amazing blessings and heart-wrenching struggles. But when we choose to look for all that we are grateful for, our mindset shifts and we focus on the positive rather than the negative.

As positivity spread like wildfire across the Twittersphere, I could feel my mindset shifting and my heart filling with joy and gratitude. I formed new friendships and felt deeper connections with those already in my professional learning family (PLF).

The #GratitudeSnaps Challenge was met with such a positive response; we decided to bring back the challenge periodically throughout the year and keep the hashtag alive by posting to it as we share our gratitude.

Gratitude is a powerful thing, and our world needs more of it. Focus on the positive in your life and the world around you, and you will be amazed at how it will reframe your thinking and shift your focus to the things that are most important in your life. Gratitude is contagious. When we model gratitude in our classrooms, our students begin to reframe their thinking and express gratitude themselves. What an important lesson we have the opportunity to teach.

Watch Your Words

Imagine what our real neighborhoods would be like if each of us offered, as a matter of course, just one kind word to another person. There have been so many stories about the lack of courtesy, the impatience of today's world, road rage, and even restaurant rage. Sometimes, all it takes is one kind word to nourish another person. Think of the ripple effect that can be created when we nourish someone. One kind empathetic word has a wonderful way of turning into many.

—Fred Rogers

In fifth grade, a shy, sensitive student took a huge risk by joining an elective music class. She had always wanted to play an instrument, specifically the flute. As she listened to the teacher talk about each instrument and what would be learned, all she could do was stare at the shiny silver flute sitting on the table. It was so pretty and made such a beautiful sound. The teacher wrapped up his introduction and called each student up by name to pick out his or her instrument. The little girl with almond-shaped eyes and a mouth full of crooked teeth could hardly wait to pick up the flute. As she approached the table that displayed the assortment of instruments, she gently picked up the flute and excitedly told the teacher that this was the instrument she wanted to play. That excitement quickly turned to embarrassment and horror as the teacher said these words, "Your lips aren't the right shape for a flute; you are better suited for the trumpet." Devastated, she grabbed the trumpet that the teacher held out for her and quickly returned to her seat where those around her snickered. As she sat down with the clunky brass trumpet on her lap, she fought back tears. Not only was this instrument not at all the one she wanted to play, but all she could think was, *What's wrong with my lips?*

The little girl with the crooked teeth and crushed heart was me. I still remember walking into the house after school that day and feigning a smile as I showed my parents the trumpet; all I wanted to do was cry. I didn't mention the comment made to me that day, but it made a lasting impact. The crazy thing was, I played that instrument all the way through my freshman year of high school, and I always hated it. I was the last chair in a row of boys who were never nice to me, and I'd always leave class with a ring around my lips, trying so hard to get that instrument to play the right note.

Looking back now, I think about how crazy it was that I endured an activity for so long that I despised. Perhaps I did so because I wanted to fit in. Regardless, the trumpet never became my passion, and a passing comment changed the way I thought about myself. I can guarantee my elementary music teacher had no idea how much his comment stuck with me throughout my adolescent years. He had no intention of it being hurtful; he probably just had an overabundance of girls who wanted to play the flute and wanted some variety.

I wonder how often I have made a flippant comment or decision out of convenience or haste without any regard to how it may be perceived. What comments have I made throughout my teaching experience that were taken out of context or received in an unintended way? Our words are powerful. We don't realize sometimes the influence we have as teachers or the lasting impact of our words. It is imperative that we model kindness in every interaction and word we speak. My fifth-grade music teacher didn't intend to be unkind; I know that—now. But his words were thoughtless. In other words, he didn't think of their impact before he spoke them. And I get that. It's easy to speak carelessly out of frustration, anger, weariness, or simply out of a desire to push our agenda, like adding a girl to the trumpet section. Each word has a potential to tear down or uplift, so we must choose each word carefully.

The importance of cultivating a culture of kindness in a classroom cannot be overstated. If we want to create classroom environments where students feel safe and are empowered to courageously pursue their passions, we need to make sure that kindness is the primary language spoken. From the very first day to the last, I express to my students the need for our classroom to be a place where kindness is expressed verbally and nonverbally. Our course is collaborative and requires all students to work together in harmony. Criticism, hate, and hostility destroy the community we work so hard to build. Kindness, expressed through words of gratitude, love, and inspiration, helps create the culture we need for all of us to succeed.

When We Share Our Fails

Often out of periods of losing come the greatest strivings toward a new winning streak.

–Fred Rogers

I opened this book with a story about our Amazing Food Truck Launch where student teams presented their recipes and business plans to potential investors. This has become a meaningful and valuable experience for my students, but things didn't go so smoothly the first time I tried this activity—and I ended up learning a few lessons myself.

I had invited staff in as "investors" to listen to food truck teams launch their concepts and taste their signature dishes. As investors came in the door, I handed them a clipboard with evaluation rubrics and $2,000 of play money. Students set up at stations in the courtyard outside my classroom with their signature dishes. Each team had an iPad that they used to show their promotional video trailers and presentations as well as a container to hold the money that investors would be allocating to the teams that they felt were most deserving.

Investors visited each team's station, listened to the pitches, tasted their delicious dishes, and provided feedback as they evaluated the students' efforts based on the rubrics. Being our first challenge, students were late getting their dishes out, which made the end of the period rushed. After the last team presented, the investors hurriedly allocated their $2,000 to the teams—seed money that would launch our food trucks on a virtual race across the United States to learn about regional cuisine.

As I was counting the money and reviewing feedback and evaluation forms from the investors, I realized that the money allocations didn't necessarily match up to the point totals on the rubric. The rankings for all but the top two teams were different. I had to make a judgment call. Would I stick with the original plan of using the currency to determine the team's ranking or use the tallied scores on the rubrics instead?

Five minutes before the next day's class began, I was still unsure of how to handle the situation. That's when I realized it was silly to keep stressing about the situation—I needed to involve the students in the problem-solving process. As students came in, I explained the dilemma and asked for their thoughts. Within just a few minutes, it was clear what needed to be done. I would eliminate the currency and base the team's ranking on the rubric scores. I immediately felt good about the decision because the teams were all in agreement; additionally, students appreciated the fact that I asked for their input. Making them part of the decision-making process made them feel valued and even more invested in the experience.

Sometime after this debacle, I shared the experience with someone from my personal learning network (PLN). Later he told me, "I appreciate that you shared about your pitfalls. Hearing how things don't work is just as important as hearing how everything is wildly successful." His statement really resonated with me because, although we talk about the importance of taking risks and the value of failure, it's not often that we share our failures. We are eager to share what's awesome about our classes and lessons, but rarely do we share the things that didn't work. The problem with this one-sided sharing is that we forget that every teacher has bad days. In the midst of epic successes, there are also epic fails. We all have days where we are discouraged, frustrated, and less than inspired.

Observing things that aren't going right in another teacher's classroom is sometimes more encouraging to me than seeing things that are. It makes me feel normal to learn that the people I follow and admire are just like me—human. It's like going over to someone's house for dinner and finding their house is less than perfect. If they have a pile of laundry on the couch or a stack of mail on the counter, it makes me relax and realize that not only is it okay to not have everything perfectly in place, but the person is comfortable enough with me to be real. I am much more likely to invite that person over for dinner, knowing that it would be okay if I had a pile of laundry on the couch too.

As innovative educators, we are all taking leaps and pushing boundaries, sometimes with huge success, sometimes with failure; nonetheless, we keep pushing forward and breaking down barriers to bring the very best teaching and learning to the classroom. Let's share our wins as well as our fails. Hearing about what doesn't go right in the classroom may be just what someone needs to realize they are not alone. And you might even get some input that helps you take another leap forward.

It's You I Like

If you can picture a female version of Mr. Rogers, that's my mom. She is a beautiful soul who raised my two siblings and me with unconditional love. Mom helped us to see the beauty in our unique qualities and gave us freedom to explore and create, all the while showering us with affirmation. She taught us it was okay to be sensitive and to embrace empathy as a special gift. She gave me courage to be myself and express my feelings. A song she would often sing to me growing up was "It's You I Like" by Fred Rogers. The song lyrics express the value of our own uniqueness. It doesn't matter what we wear, our hairstyle, or what's deep inside us; our skin, eyes, and feelings are worthy of being liked.

I grew up knowing that, no matter what, I was liked just the way I was. No personality quirk, poor decision, hurts, failures, or outward and inward characteristics would ever alter that. Now as an adult, I realize how much those words have stuck with me. More importantly, they taught me to like myself, truly appreciate the uniqueness and gifts I'd been given. Maybe my mom realized that my learning to like myself was actually one of the most important lessons of all. As a person with highly sensitive, intuitive personality traits, I've always been my worst critic. Throughout all of life's ups and downs, failures, and disappointments, my mom has always expressed her belief in me when I had difficulty believing in myself. Without the solid foundation of love and acceptance growing up, I don't know how I would have navigated through life.

> **As human beings, our job in life is to help people realize how rare and valuable each one of us really is, that each of us has something that no one else has–or ever will have–something inside that is unique to all time. It's our job to encourage each other to discover that uniqueness and to provide ways of developing its expression.**
>
> **–Fred Rogers**

As an adult, I am painfully aware that not all children are raised with as nurturing a mom as I am blessed to have; however, I view every student who comes into my class as an opportunity to give back some of what I was so richly lavished with as a child. I want them to experience complete and utter love and acceptance and to know that they each hold a unique combination of personality traits, gifts, talents, and skills that make them special. I want them to know that I am there to support and help them reach their full potential, that I believe in them.

We are given moments—incredible opportunities—to make a tremendous imprint on human hearts. These moments shape who they believe themselves to be. In the words of my childhood hero, Fred Rogers, "In the external scheme of things, shining moments are as brief as the twinkling of an eye, yet such twinklings are what eternity is made of—moments when we human beings can say, 'I love you,' 'I'm proud of you,' 'I forgive you,' 'I'm grateful for you.' That's what eternity is made of: invisible, imperishable, good stuff."

Let Your Students Shine

Some teachers and students start getting ready for summer break as the school year winds down. That has never been my experience. For the past eleven years, the end of the school year means getting ready to cater Senior Boards. Senior Boards are two days at the end of the school year where students give their senior project speeches in front of a panel of judges comprised of staff and community members. It's a day my students anticipate and prepare for with months of hard work.

Our culinary department has always had the honor of catering this event by serving savory and sweet delicacies, all lovingly prepared by all levels of our culinary students. It's a huge undertaking to say the least. We spend two weeks planning and preparing food for this event to make sure it is a special and delicious spread for our seniors. After eleven years of catering this event, I had it pretty much dialed in. I had detailed ingredient lists and plans of how to organize the preparation and storage. It was a well-oiled machine, and I was in control. I knew what students would make, the exact quantities for each item, and who would make them. Students have always followed through with the plan and impressed me with the quality food they produced. Recently, however, I realized something: In taking control, I was preventing my students from owning this experience. Sure, they were making amazing food, but they were working from my ideas, my plan. The students were just going through the motions. A well-oiled machine is great, but if the students aren't operating the machine, there is a problem. Were they learning? Yes. Were they empowered? No.

So what did I do? I decided to hand over control and threw out some of the recipes we had always made so that my students could have some agency over the planning. Culinary 1 and 2 made some of our tried-and-true recipes that staff and community members always look forward to, but I gave my Culinary 3 and 4 students complete control over what to serve. In Culinary 3, each food truck team planned a table with food, showcasing their final destination in their journey across the United States: the Pacific Northwest. Teams planned dishes, calculated the ingredient quantities needed to serve to more than seven hundred people, and designed their table presentation. Culinary 4 students came up with their own menu to serve what would showcase their skills.

In addition to giving students more agency over the preparation and planning, we changed the venue and layout of how food was served to allow for students to be at each of the stations and communicate with the guests. There was also a station set up for guests to vote on their favorite food truck, so I could determine the final winners of our Amazing Food Truck Race.

Let me tell you, relinquishing that control was super scary! This was more than taking a risk that would only affect the students in my classroom. This risk could impact a long-standing tradition at South Medford High School. Community judges and staff members look forward to the refreshments every year at this event that celebrates our seniors' accomplishments. I really didn't want this idea to fail.

Even after setting things in motion, there were moments when I second-guessed my sanity. Losing control is hard. It's uncertain. It's risky. One day during those two weeks when I was feeling especially out of control, I came to a realization while walking around my class: My kids were the ones in control. They all knew what they needed to do, and they were getting it done. Even better, they were excited! They *owned* this experience and were empowered to make it the best they possibly could. They knew they were going to be serving their dishes to their peers, teachers, staff, and community members, and they wanted to impress them all!

At the event, my students completely shined! They set up beautiful displays, acted professionally, and served incredible food. I received numerous comments from guests on how impressed they were with the quality of their food and their professionalism. I even heard feedback that they could tell my students were empowered. Taking this huge risk reminded me that it is okay to be scared. Traditions are great, but sometimes they need a little shaking up. Losing control can be a good thing, especially when doing so empowers students to shine!

Ask the Students

Part of what made the Senior Board event so successful is that the students had agency over their work. In addition to control over their learning, students want to connect their learning to their own personal experiences. That's what makes learning relevant and meaningful. When we allow the opportunity for students to make these connections, they find value in what they are learning, and they become more willing and even excited to continue exploring.

Recently I had an opportunity to sit and chat with a group of high school students about meaningful learning, and *wow*, I loved hearing their incredible insight. Here's what they said:

* Teachers should provide more hands-on activities for students who need and want to understand better.
* Students get bored by doing nothing. When a teacher leaves time unfilled in class, students play on their phones, talk to their friends, or sleep. I want less down time and more learning time.
* Talk to the quiet students on a personal level, making sure they understand the problem. Don't necessarily call on them: just walk over and talk to them one-on-one.
* Yes, taking notes is important, but once students are done jotting them down, they won't look at them until next class. I want to leave class saying, "Wow, I didn't know that!"
* Students need to learn everyday activities such as how to file taxes, balance checking accounts, buy a car or house, or pay bills. They need to know the difference between debit and credit cards and taking out loans. I want to be prepared for the real world.
* Some teachers aren't excited about teaching, which makes class boring, and no one enjoys the class. If teachers were more happy and cheerful, it would make the class more interesting. We understand there are bad days, but we have a hard time paying attention when we aren't interested.
* Students are normally compliant, and that's how teachers like it, but we should change up the way things are taught for different ways of thinking. Is there a way teachers can change up the thinking/teaching process since everyone learns differently?

We try so hard to figure out the best strategies to engage students in meaningful learning, but how often do we ask them how they want to learn? How often do we really listen to what they have to say? When these students started talking about learning, they were passionate. They want to learn. They know how important it is for their future. What an honor we have to educate our youth and to make a lasting impact on how they view learning. We need to listen to our kids; they have a lot to teach us that can help teachers make better connections to the learning for our students.

Create Circumstances for Authenticity and Agency

When we create circumstances for authenticity and agency, our classrooms become magical places full of empowered learners. This intentional shift of mindset and approach to how we interact with our students and learning in our classroom can make a profound and lasting impact.

- ✳ What is one thing you are grateful for right now? How can you show your appreciation? Consider doing a thirty-day gratitude challenge with your students.
- ✳ When is the last time you tried something new and failed? Did you tell anyone about the experience? Will you?
- ✳ How can you tap into your students' passions?
- ✳ What can you do to ensure the students in your classroom feel confident enough to pursue their authentic passions?
- ✳ How can you tap into your own passions and bring your best teaching and learning to the classroom each day?
- ✳ How can you make learning come alive for every kid who steps into your class?

Chapter 4

Gamified Experiences

When I met Michael Matera in a lunch line at a Miami conference back in 2014, I was already a fan of playing games and using gamifying strategies. I knew about points and badges, but as we talked, I realized Michael's approach went beyond those strategies to create an immersive, play-filled learning environment. I immediately made connections of this idea of gamification to some of the gamified strategies I used in my class. My student's *loved* when I infused "Chopped" and "Mystery Box" challenges; in fact, they were always begging me to do it more often. With this concept of gamification, games wouldn't just be an "every once in a while" occurrence, but play would be an element of an overarching class theme. My mind began spinning with the possibilities, and I went home and started planning how I could gamify my own classroom.

When I began gamifying my classes three years ago, I had no idea of the amazing adventure it would take me on. For each of my culinary classes, I create a storyline that frames my curriculum and integrates game mechanics to encourage interactive, playful, and challenging learning. In Culinary 3, for example, students are learning about American Regional Cuisine. I created a storyline based on a Great Food Truck Race theme and teams of students are on a race across America to learn about the flavor and profiles of our country's cuisine. The immersive learning environment that has been created by this new way of teaching and learning has transformed my classroom into one that is bursting with creativity, collaboration, problem solving, and critical thinking. I truly can't imagine going back to the way I taught class before.

As I share my gamified experiences in this chapter to follow, I want to again thank Michael for his influence and inspiration and for his must-read book, *Explore Like a Pirate.* His philosophy of gamification has transformed the way I look at teaching and learning. In my classroom today, we experience more fun and adventure. The students experience intense learning, but the focus is less on grades and more on empowering them to take hold of their educational experience. We do that through *gamification.*

Gamification Deconstructed

There are a lot of varying perspectives on what gamification is and what it can look like in a classroom. Michael describes gamification as "taking the most motivational techniques of games and applying them to non-game settings, like classrooms." Often people confuse gamification and game-based learning. Although it's true that gamification uses elements of games to engage students, game-based learning uses games to meet learning objectives. There are a lot of opportunities to bring game-based learning into the gamified class, but they are not one and the same.

Gamification doesn't mean you start from scratch or redesign your curriculum. It's a framework that works with your existing curriculum to enhance what you already do. When you gamify, you layer the motivational elements of games over your curriculum to create an immersive learning environment. Gamification is far more than tacking on XP points or badges. It creates a rich experience where learning truly comes alive in a magical way for your students. It's engaging and challenging and so fun that your students will run into class with anticipation of what the day will bring.

I love this quote from Michael: "The power of play brings back the natural yearning that exists inside all of us to learn." It doesn't matter if we are young or old. Something magical happens when we play. It awakens the child within all of us. So consider this: What games bring out the playful spirit in you? Maybe you love board games, such as Sorry, Scrabble, Life, or Catan. How about cards? Do you enjoy playing Hearts, Solitaire, or Progressive Rummy? Video games may be what really piques your interest; you could stay up to the wee hours of the night playing Call of Duty or Mario Bros. Neither of those game styles appeal to you? How about game apps? Are you on Level 356 of Candy Crush or Panda Pop? Or maybe you love the more social game apps like Words with Friends. Still not tapping into your playful spirit? Do you love sports? Basketball? Baseball? Football? Golf? Once you find the game or game category that appeals to you, ask yourself the following:

- What do I enjoy about those games?
- What can I learn from them?
- What are the motivational aspects of the games that get people hooked and make us want to play again and again?

With those questions in mind, let's start deconstructing games by using Monopoly as an example so that you can better understand the dynamics in play. Love it or hate it, it's a game that many are familiar with. Though many have played the game, not many have spent time thinking about the fictional storyline that gives context for the game to operate in. To better understand the storyline as it relates to game play, let's break down this American classic into theme, setting, characters, and action:

Theme: Monopoly is the theme that frames this fictional story and serves as the backdrop for the game.

Setting: Monopoly takes place on the real-life streets of Atlantic City, New Jersey.

Characters: The iconic Mr. Monopoly is the top-hat-wearing man with the mustache and cane whom many associate with the game. The players, represented by metal tokens, are real estate tycoons purchasing and developing increasingly expensive property in hopes of controlling the market; additionally, there is a banker who distributes assets from the bank to the players throughout the game as they are acquired.

Action: The challenges and obstacles that players encounter throughout the game contribute to the game's action. By the luck of a good draw, you may collect $50 because of the "Grand Opera Opening" or, less fortunately, get sent to jail by an opponent and have to stay there until you roll doubles. Adding opportunities for chance and choice keeps players immersed and adds a level of excitement. There is always that chance that good fortune will come your way but also the possibility of getting a string of bad luck that will slow you down.

Now that we've looked at what draws us into the story of Monopoly, let me introduce you to the mechanics that are at play within the game and keep us hooked for hours on end. Game mechanics tell us how to play the game and are broken down into rules, strategies, and goals.

The ***rules*** of Monopoly consist of rolling dice, moving your character around the game board, paying rent, and collecting cards and property. The ***strategy*** involves trying to buy as many streets as possible within a color grouping so that you have the opportunity to purchase homes and hotels and profit from the other players in the game. The ***goal*** is to end the game with more money than all the other players. Break those down even further and you have all of the individual mechanics that keep the game exciting: dice, Community Chest cards, Chance cards, currency, property, railroads, free parking, jail, homes, and houses.

Maybe you are thinking, "These mechanics don't keep me hooked! I don't enjoy playing Monopoly till the wee hours of the night; in fact, I don't like the game!" If that's you, consider what game mechanic you could add to make it more engaging for you. Did you know that there is a rule that is often overlooked in the directions? According to the official Monopoly game rules, a property goes to auction if the player that lands on it doesn't want to buy it. The rules state, "If you do not wish to buy the property, the Banker sells it at auction to the highest bidder. The buyer pays the Bank the amount of the bid in cash and receives the Title Deed card for that property." The addition of this simple rule could change everything for the Monopoly hater. Not only would it speed up the game, but the auction gives players the opportunities to buy property at a discount. It also adds strategy, as the person who landed on the space can decide to send it to auction and then buy it for less. The beauty of game mechanics is that you can create rules, strategies, and goals for your classroom game that hook even the most reluctant learner. If the game isn't good, make it better!

What are the aspects of Monopoly you enjoy? Are you one who loves being immersed in the storyline and the social interaction with the other players? Or maybe you find the strategizing and acquisition of property to be the most fun part of the game.

What can we learn from this game structure that we could bring into our classroom? Are there opportunities to add elements of chance, choice, and challenge in student learning? Can you create unique opportunities that allow for strategy and exploration of your curriculum?

What are the motivational aspects of the game that hook us and make us want to play again and again? Often these are the same aspects that make us enjoy the game, but without them, we wouldn't be likely to play for extended lengths of time. Some players may be motivated by the excitement and unpredictability of rolling the dice or drawing a Chance card? The challenging obstacles, unique opportunities, or the sense of achievement from acquiring property and currency may be what keep others in the game into the wee hours of the night.

Think about the kids you know: the students in your classroom or your own kids at home. What games hold their attention? What draws them in and keeps them captivated for hours on end? As Dr. Bobb Darnell, president of Achievement Strategies, Incorporated, states, "Kids will play a video game on average of one hundred hours just to 'get good' at it. They don't get grades, extra credit, win money, or get public acclaim. Yet they rarely play that game a second time without knowing/learning objectives and goals, strategies and skills, vocabulary, how well they are doing, or what to do better next time." How can we tap into that desire to improve? How can we harness the motivation that keeps our students up far past their bedtimes to play their favorite video game and bring it into the classroom? You may already be predicting the answer is "gamify" but are wondering how you would go about it. Stay tuned because, in the section ahead, I will share with you exactly how I designed my gamified classroom structure.

Words of Advice

When I returned from Miami in the Winter of 2014, I knew I had to wrap my head around this idea of gamification. To be completely honest, I felt overwhelmed at first and didn't know where to start. After just one quarter of gamifying my classroom, however, I was hooked. I knew that this was something that I needed to develop further. The degree of collaboration, problem solving, critical thinking, and creativity that was happening was exciting. Students were more motivated to learn than I'd ever witnessed before and were doing more than was even required. I loved that they were having fun in the process! When that quarter ended, I knew that this was only the beginning. The following year, I expanded my gamification to Culinary Arts 3 in the first semester, and by the second semester, I had gamified all of my Culinary 2 classes as well.

Start Small

Some teachers like to dive in headfirst and gamify everything all at once. That's fine if it works for you, but remember that it is okay to start small. You don't have to completely gamify your entire class from the onset. Start with a unit that you would like to revamp. Maybe it's one that you really don't enjoy teaching, or it has lost its excitement. What could you do to breathe life into it for you and your students? If a semester or unit seems overwhelming, start with a lesson. When I first began, I took it slow and decided to just gamify one class for one quarter. I felt like this was a manageable place to start. The point is, do what works best for you.

Allow the Game to Evolve over Time

I started simple and added new mechanics, twists, and turns as I went. Starting small and evolving the game over time not only saves my sanity starting out, it also allows for creative ideas to flow organically and keeps the game exciting for my students; additionally, I ask them what changes or new elements they would like to see. Doing so gives them a voice and benefits me. Some of my very best game additions have come from my students.

You Can Start without It All Figured Out

It's important to understand that I didn't have the MasterChef, Great Food Truck Race, and Amazing Race games all figured out from the beginning. My games have always been a work in progress that have developed through play. If I had waited till it was all planned and perfect, it would have never happened. Honestly, even if it had been planned out, most likely, I would have made changes.

Your students will guide you as they respond to the game. Seeing your students' enthusiasm is addicting and will make you want to look for ways to add in game mechanics.

Gamification Can Work in Any Content Area or Grade Level

I have seen gamification transform classrooms at every grade level and in a variety of content areas. The creative options and game designs you can use to make learning magical in your classroom are endless. If it can transform a unique class like culinary arts, it can transform your classroom too!

Designing Your Game

The biggest challenge for me when beginning to gamify was where to start; it was overwhelming to say the least. Though I loved the idea of creating a gamified learning environment, I wasn't sure how to set it up.

Find Your Inspiration

What do you love? Maybe you are an avid reader and are especially fond of a particular book or series. Do you love movies? Are you a fanatic about the outdoors, games, or television reality shows? Once you figure out what your inspiration is, begin immersing yourself in that world. Take notes as you consider what it is that you love about your inspiration point. What stands out? What elements can you bring into your classroom?

Create a Basic Game Plan

As a visual learner, I knew I would need something to organize my ideas visually, so I could see my game taking shape. I developed a basic game plan that helped me organize my game structure and made sense of all the ideas spinning in my mind. This game plan has allowed each game to build naturally as my students learn and interact with the game. It also enables me to personalize the games based on the interests and needs of my students. On the next page is an example of my MasterChef Game Plan that I created in Google Drawings. This framework gives structure to my game and gives me a launching pad to start building in game mechanics to motivate and empower.

MASTERCHEF

STORY

SETTING: My room is transformed into the MasterChef Kitchen

CHARACTER: Students are aspiring chefs on a mission to acquire new culinary skills and earn 3 Michelin stars by the end of the semester.

ACTION: Students participate in Mystery Box Challenges, Mini Games, and our MasterChef Challenge at the end of the unit. I break down each in more detail as I explain my game mechanics.

GOAL: Students are on a quest each unit to become MasterChef by earning 4000 XP. They earn a Michelin star each time they earn Masterchef status. The ultimate goal is to earn 3 Michelin stars before the end of the semester.

GAME MECHANICS

LEVELS Students can earn XP a variety of ways throughout each unit to level up and earn certain privileges.

Apprentice: 1000 XP	May use 3x5 on unit test
Sous Chef: 2000 XP	May partner with a Sous Chef OR use full page of notes on test
MasterChef: 4000 XP	Exempt from unit test Free Cooking Day Michelin Star

BADGES Students have an opportunity to earn tangible badges for demonstrating their learning in various ways throughout unit.

CHANCE CARDS Chance Cards are put into a box, and when I notice students demonstrating extraordinary employability skills, I allow them to randomly grab a card from the box.

BAKERY MISSIONS Missions give students an opportunity to demonstrate their understanding of the content—above and beyond what they do in class. Missions are always related to the essential questions of the unit, are never given a grade, and always have an expiration date.

MINI GAMES Variety of digital and analog games played throughout the unit for formative assessment and review.

MASTERCHEF CHALLENGES At the end of each unit, I take an essential skill that they learned and ask them to demonstrate it without a recipe and make it something delicious.

Developing Your Story

After reading *Explore Like a Pirate*, I was fully convinced that the magic of the gamified class begins with story. As explained in my deconstruction of the game of Monopoly, developing a storyline will bring context to your game and make it come to life. I am going to break down each of Michael's elements for you first and then share what this looks like in each of my game designs.

Theme

I will never forget the advice Michael Matera gave me when I first began this adventure: "Find a theme, and everything will start falling into place." This advice has rung true in every unit and class I have gamified.

Think of an overarching theme you could layer over your existing curriculum, and the planning process will magically be set into motion. It just so happened that about the time I started gamifying, I was leaving for a three-day conference and planned on showing the movie *The Hundred-Foot Journey* that connected to standards we were going to be learning in class. When thinking about the storyline, I realized it could be a great theme for a game. In the movie, the main character is chasing after his passion for cooking and is on a mission to earn three Michelin Stars in the process. I had found my starting point! Students would be on a quest to earn three Michelin Stars.

As you consider your storyline, determine what the goal of your game will be. What are they working towards? What are you hoping students accomplish?

Setting

Once I had a theme in place, I brainstormed about what that world would be like. How could I transform my classroom in a way that made students feel as if they were being transported to another place? My setting has developed over time, and because I teach more than one subject and have more than one game going, I don't do a lot of decorating for the theme; however, when students step into my classroom, they know they have entered another world, and they are excited to be a part of it. Each day, my color-coded kitchens are transformed into the MasterChef kitchen, a food truck, or a restaurant in another part of the world. Some days, theme music plays in the background, and special instructions on the projector screen lead to a clue. Another day, there may be mystery boxes full of secret ingredients that students will use to create a dish in a timed challenge. They aren't just walking into room D108; they are stepping into a story designed for them.

Characters

Once your setting is established, you can begin thinking about the characters. Who is in this game? Who will your students be in the game? What other characters are involved, either real or fictional? My students immerse themselves in the storyline by becoming characters in the game. On special challenge days, our staff, restaurant owners, and community members become guests that step into the game as judges, investors, or customers.

Action

The last aspect of developing your story comes with the action. How will your story come to life? Will there be secret missions, battles, or adventures? How could you rename some of the things you already do to connect with your theme? What are some new activities, games, or challenges that would take your content to another level? I always incorporate action in my game at the end of a unit when we have our challenges; however, there are also other activities and mini games that I incorporate within each unit to add action as well. I love building curiosity and suspense by surprising students with a new activity that they weren't expecting. Keeping the game dynamic by incorporating fresh ideas keeps students on their toes and engaged in the classroom experience.

Game Mechanics

Now that you have your story in place, you can start adding in game mechanics that will set your game in motion. As mentioned before, the game mechanics indicate how your game is played and involve the rules, strategy, and goal. I think of this as an immersive framework layered over the curriculum in which my game world operates. The mechanics change in each game that I've created. There are mechanics established when the game is launched; however, the rules and strategies can change while the game is in play. Again, you don't have to start the game having everything figured out. Pay attention to how your students are responding and adjust accordingly. Here are a few of the game mechanics I have incorporated in my classroom that have powerfully impacted my classroom culture:

Badges and Experience Points

As students demonstrate an understanding of the skills and essential questions in my classroom, they have the opportunity to earn badges and accumulate experience points, a.k.a. XP. These baseball-card-size badges can be stored in a plastic sheet. The badges hold various amounts of XP that can help students progress to various levels in the game.

Levels

Creating levels for students to reach with their XP is a wonderful way to immerse and engage the students in each unit and empower them to own their learning. With each level reached, students earn various privileges that give them advantages in the game. Students can earn XP as they level up, something I find makes them more focused on the learning, which leads to better retention of the content. I also have found that levels allow me to differentiate the learning experience for students. Those who typically don't do well on tests have an opportunity to demonstrate their understanding in other ways.

Product Quality

In my culinary classes, product quality is important—everyone likes good food and a beautiful presentation. I use lab experiences as an opportunity for students to collaborate as a team, to acquire a new skill, and to make something amazing. Before a lab, I explain that an exemplary product is a restaurant- or bakery-quality product that I would pay money for.

Student teams then head to their kitchens on a mission. This is not an assignment or a requirement that they must complete. This is a quest for mastery, an opportunity to do the extraordinary. At the end of the lab, when students bring me their product, they come with a look of anticipation and pride on their faces. They all owned this experience, and they can't wait to find out what I think of their creations. To evaluate, I give teams a score of one to five for taste, texture, and appearance. I ask them guiding questions—to help them problem solve and think through the steps that resulted in the product's quality—and give them descriptive feedback. Teams that score the highest quality in that day's lab receive a product quality badge of 500XP. Every student who participated on the team that day earns this badge.

Missions

Missions give students an opportunity to demonstrate their understanding of the content—above and beyond what they do in class. Missions are always related to the essential questions of the unit, are never given a grade, and always have an expiration date. Typically, I launch one mission for each essential question in the unit. I don't create strict criteria. I want these missions to allow for creativity and agency. I find that when I give students the opportunity to create, they blow my mind! When we limit creativity to little boxes, they stick to those constraints. But when we open the lids to those boxes and tell them the sky's the limit, they shoot for the stars.

It is incredible what students will do for XP that they won't do for a grade. Presentation is everything. I could ask students to do homework, attach a grade to it, and students would view it as work; instead, I call it a mission and challenge them to do something outstanding for XP, and they view it as fun and exciting.

It is also important to think about the point of the mission. Are we asking them to simply regurgitate information or to think deeply about the content, solve problems, and create something powerful with it? Students don't want to do meaningless tasks. They want to be challenged; they want learning to have meaningful purpose.

Chance Cards

When I established my MasterChef game, I was really happy with the structure. The storyline came together, and the game mechanics I had set in motion were effective; however, I found that a few students who seemed to enjoy the class weren't necessarily motivated by the game mechanics like everyone else. The beauty of the gamified class is that *you* are the game designer. You can add twists and turns in the game any time you want. When I observed how my students were reacting to the game and realized some hadn't bought in like the others, I decided to create another game mechanic to draw them in: Chance Cards. I made a list of all of the things that students were always asking to do and then created a card for each that would give them permission to do it.

Think about the students in your classroom. What is something they are always asking to do? This will vary greatly depending on the subject and grade that you teach. Let me get you started with some possibilities, and soon your mind will be swirling with ideas!

Here are some Chance Card examples:

- **Exit Early:** Leave class two minutes early.
- **Coffee Card:** One free trip to the coffee bar (Keurig cup)
- **Mix It Up:** Free mix-in ingredient for an upcoming lab
- **Double Whammy:** Double your recipe.
- **Freezing Time:** Two-day extension on a mission
- **Sabotage:** Take one ingredient from a team in a challenge.
- **Boomerang:** When presented with a sabotage, this card will bounce it back to the team who gave it.
- **Block:** A block prevents another team from giving you a sabotage.
- **Let the Music Play:** Select the music played in class for the day.
- **Teacher's Pet:** Ask the teacher to eliminate one multiple choice option from a test question.
- **Switcheroo:** Switch seats with another student for the day.
- **Dog Ate My Homework:** Use this excuse for one homework assignment.
- **Eat Lunch with Teacher:** Choose a friend to join you for a lunch in class with the teacher.
- **Chair Swap:** Swap chairs with the teacher for the day.
- **Cross It Off:** Cross out a test question of choice.

Mini Games

Mini games are a powerful component to the gamified classroom. They can be used for learning new terminology, formative assessments, unit review, incorporating a brain break, or infusing some fun and laughter when energy is low and stress is high. I love the flexibility and adaptability of mini games. You can vary the length, change the rules, and make up your own! The possibilities are truly endless!

There are many digital games like Kahoot!, Quizizz, Quizlet Live, and Gimkit that allow you to create games that are available to use whenever you need them. Many digital games also have premade games categorized by content area that you can save and modify based on your curriculum.

One digital game that my students love is called Gimkit. Once teachers create a kit, students log on to the site from any device and enter a four-digit code and their name. This digital review tool allows students to answer questions on a device at their own pace. One wonderful feature of this tool is that students will get exposure to the questions multiple times to ensure mastery. The game feature that my students really enjoy is the opportunity to earn in-game cash by answering questions. The more questions students answer correctly, the more earning potential they have. To hook them even more, there is strategy involved. When players earn a certain amount of money, they are able to "upgrade" by reinvesting their money. This powerful mechanic allows students to play to their strengths with over four thousand different upgrade combinations! This is a game my students want to play again and again. To make it even better, it was created by a student, and there are new improvements and mechanics being continually built into the game!

Another longtime favorite is Kahoot! The game allows you to digitally build banks of questions on specific topics and gives many options for play. You can have students play individually or as a team. Once you create your question banks, you can easily start a game without any advance preparation. It's the perfect way to formatively assess your students on review days and when you have a little extra time in class. When we play, I give XP to the top scorers whether that is a team of students or an individual. One of the best aspects of these mini games is that they reward the students who have mastered the content without penalizing those who haven't. I also can download the data from the Kahoot! games onto a spreadsheet so I can track their progress.

I have also made up my own games to review skills and concepts. Once you start thinking like a game designer, there's no limit to what you can come up with! Games are not just a perfect way to review for tests of all kinds; they also bring fun, laughter, and the challenge of playful learning. I am continually on the hunt to find new games to add to my closet of ideas. Whenever I watch game shows or walk down game aisles, I am looking for ideas and inspiration to bring into our classroom adventures. Our local toy store was going out of business and had some pretty incredible discounts on their games. As I was perusing the game aisle, I did a double take. I saw the game Topple was discounted 90 percent! What?! I hadn't heard of this game, but I love a good bargain, and I knew I could find a way to use it for learning! I must admit the stack of Topple games sat there for quite some time just begging to be played. As I was planning for an upcoming review day, I glanced at the counter and decided those games needed to come to life! I made slight adjustments to the rules, and it adapted to our classroom logistics beautifully!

TOPPLE

Object of the Game

Score the most points by completing or adding to stacks or rows of playing pieces while being careful not to topple any of the other pieces.

Materials Needed

- Topple game board
- Die

- ✳ Topple pieces
- ✳ Set of review questions
- ✳ Score sheet

Set Up

- ✳ 4 islands of tables with a cup of colored Topple pieces on the middle of each
- ✳ 1 table in the middle with Topple Board and dice

Rules

1. Divide class into teams of four and have them sit at one of the four table islands.
2. Have a representative from each group come up to the middle table to roll a die. The highest roll will go first.
3. Ask the group with the highest roll a question from the review sheet and set the timer for one minute. If they answer the question correctly, one student from the team comes up to the middle table and rolls the die. The number they roll corresponds with the numbers on the Topple Board: 1=level 1, 2=level 2, etc., and 6 is wild (can be placed anywhere on the board). They place their Topple piece in a location that would keep the board balanced without toppling over.
   - ✳ 1 point for placing Topple piece on board
   - ✳ 3 points for completing a row of 5 pieces in any direction
   - ✳ Bonus point for every color that tops each stack in that row
   - ✳ 1 point for every color that tops each stack in the row of 5 for remainder of game

    - ✳ 1 point for every piece of your color in a stack of 3 or higher

    If they answer the question incorrectly, the next team to the right gets a chance to steal. If the stealing team answers correctly, they have the same opportunity to roll the die and place the Topple piece on the board. If not, the next team steals, until someone answers correctly.

4. The second question goes back to the second table, and play repeats in the same manner.
5. The first team to topple the board and have pieces fall ends the game and loses all points. The remaining teams add up their points. Teams with the highest points overall win the game.

The beauty of this game is there are endless variations to the rules. You can add your own rules and point possibilities, or better yet, ask your students to create their own rules! They love designing games and usually have better ideas than I do! Another one that I adapted for my classroom that has become a favorite is Cranium.

CRANIUM

Game Scenario

Players act, draw, sculpt, describe, and spell backwards vocabulary terms in this fun-filled game where everyone has a chance to shine!

Materials Needed

- ✳ Fifty blue index cards
- ✳ Fifty red index cards
- ✳ A pen for each team
- ✳ Two bags or bowls for vocabulary terms
- ✳ Two dice
- ✳ Two mini whiteboards or surface to draw on

- ✳ Assortment of colored dry erase markers
- ✳ Container of playdough for each team
- ✳ Two sand timers

Rules

1. Divide class into two teams. One team will be blue and the other team red.
2. Give each team the following: index cards (red team gets blue cards, blue team gets red), sand timer, die, drawing surface, playdough, and pen.
3. Have each team come up with fifty vocabulary terms that relate to the unit of study or your course curriculum. Teams will select one person to write a different term on each index card. These will be for the other team to guess.
4. The teacher can check each team's terms for accuracy and place in two different bags or bowls, one for each team.
5. When all terms have been written onto index cards and collected, teams determine who will go first by figuring out who has the closest birthday.
6. The player with the closest birthday on each team will go first by rolling the die. Highest roll indicates which team is first to play.
7. The player will roll the die, draw a card from their team's bowl, and try to get their team to guess the term using the activity indicated by the die before the sand timer runs out.
    - ✳ Roll 1: Cloodle—Draw a picture of the term on the whiteboard or paper (no talking)
    - ✳ Roll 2: Creative Cat—Sculpt the term with playdough (no talking)
    - ✳ Roll 3: Cameo—Act the term out (no talking)

- Roll 4: Listofacto—Describe it by using no more than 3 facts
- Roll 5: Grilleps—Spell term backwards
- Roll 6: Choose It—You get to pick what activity you want!

8. If the player is successful, the team keeps the card and earns a point. Then the other team has a turn. Play rotates clockwise to each team member and continues until a determined time or card amount is reached. The team with the most cards at the end of the game is the winner!

I love the flexibility of this game! It can work with any grade level and subject and can be adapted to the age levels of your learners. You can have as few or as many activities as you want, and it can be played with various-size groups. It also appeals to a wide range of learners, as there are many ways to describe the terminology. To incorporate more choice and less chance, you could let each player decide which activity they want to use.

There is something magical about the energy that is created by the games we play. Collaboration. Strategy. Chance. Laughter. Bonding. Fun. *Learning!* When we create memorable experiences for our students, the learning sticks. I challenge you to open up your game cabinet at home or spend some time wandering the game aisle at your local stores. There is so much inspiration to be found there, and the possibilities are endless! How can you take your favorite game and bring it into your classroom to create new opportunities for learning?

Challenges

Challenges are what make life interesting, and overcoming them is what makes life meaningful.

–Joshua J. Marine

Sometimes it's the simple adjustments in how we frame learning that can make the biggest impact. If you were given a choice between completing an assignment or a challenge, what would you choose? I don't know about you, but I would definitely choose the challenge. Taking an assignment that you've always done and turning it into a challenge can completely transform how your students feel about a task. There is something playful about this subtle change that immerses students and allows them to think more deeply about what they are doing. I have noticed such a transformation in how my students interact and engage during these challenges that they have become an integral part of my classroom dynamic. I love to give students multiple opportunities to prove to themselves what they are capable of. One of my favorite ways to do this is by giving them unexpected challenges. Let me share with you an example of how I incorporate challenges into my class:

Setting the Stage

As students come into the classroom, epic adventure music plays, and on the screen are the words, "Get ready! Your first MasterChef Challenge is about to begin!" Excitement immediately fills the room as the class anticipates what is to come and begins to pepper me with questions as they try to figure out what I'm about to reveal.

The Challenge Revealed!

When the final bell rings, I reveal what is about to take place. Eight folded sheets of paper are displayed on my table. I tell them that on each paper is one of two formulas for yeast bread: a rich dough and a lean dough. Each team will randomly choose one of the papers to reveal which dough they will be making for the challenge. But there is a catch! These formulas do not include instructions. They will have to collaborate as a team to prepare the dough according to the straight dough method that they've been taught without any instructions to rely on; additionally, they will be making this dough into something extraordinary and all their own! The challenge has barely begun, and already the wheels are turning in my students' minds as each team begins to strategize their plan of action.

An Unexpected Twist

Wait! There's more! Once all teams have selected their formula, I unveil an assortment of ingredients displayed on the counter and reveal another twist to the challenge. I hand each team some foam dice, which they will roll to determine how many mix-in ingredients they get to add in to their dough. If they roll two, they get two ingredients; if they roll four, they get four, etc. As each team rolls the dice, you can hear a pin drop. They can't wait to see what the dice will reveal!

The Challenge Begins

Once all the teams have rolled, the challenge can begin. The timer on the board lets students know it's time to enter their kitchens to get to work. Students spend the rest of the period preparing their dough and planning out their creation. They will have half of the period on the following day to shape, bake, and present their creations. As they work, I love to walk around the room and listen to all the chatter and learning in action. The room buzzes with creativity, communication, collaboration, and critical thinking of students completely immersed in learning. Each member of the team is essential in the success of this challenge, and they know it!

MasterChef Challenge—Part 2

Students practically run in on the second day of the challenge. They can't wait to get started shaping and baking their dough into something mind-blowing! I give students about forty-five minutes to finish their preparation before the judging begins. For this challenge, I have my student aide "Sous Chef" and staff members help in the judging. We set up a judging table where we evaluate their creations based on taste, texture, appearance, and creativity according to a five-point scale. We will tally the score sheets, and the first place team will earn 1,000 XP, second place, 750 XP, and third place, 500 XP.

The Empowered Learner

As students bring up their creations one by one, their faces say it all. They are so proud of what they've created. They are empowered learners who just took their knowledge and made it their own in the most epic way. They were challenged beyond what they thought they could do, and they not only did it, but they *crushed* it! This is the ultimate form of assessment, and yet they never think about it that way. During this challenging and fun experience, they were so immersed in the process they didn't realize what was really happening here: they were demonstrating to me what they had learned!

There are so many challenges we can adapt from reality shows like *Cutthroat Kitchen*, *Amazing Race*, and *Shark Tank*. Spend a day binge watching some of the many shows on television and your mind will be bursting with ideas. Here are a few challenge ideas that I love. They are, of course, outlined for my culinary classroom, but you can adapt the concepts to any subject matter.

Mystery Box Challenge

Place ingredients in a box on each team's counter. When the timer starts, students remove the items and use them to prepare a dish in the time given. Dishes are evaluated based on taste, texture, and creativity.

Variation for English Language-Arts Class: Instead of ingredients, place objects in a box. When the timer starts, reveal the objects to the class and have them write a short story about the objects revealed.

Recipe Relay Challenge

Give teams an envelope that contains strips of paper with recipe ingredients and steps on them. When the timer starts, teams have to sort the recipe steps into the correct order. One team member at a time enters the kitchen and begins following the recipe. After a determined amount of time, I say, "switch," and another team member taps in and continues where the last team member left off. This continues until all team members have tapped in at least once and the recipe has been completed.

Variation for Foreign Language Class: Instead of strips of paper containing recipe steps, they are instructions for completing a task written in a foreign language. Just as above, teams have to sort steps into the right order and take turns following steps until the task is completed.

Name That Recipe

Also known as a Road Block in the Amazing Race game, Name that Recipe is a challenge that involves a recipe that is missing its title. Students follow the recipe instructions to prepare the recipe while trying to figure out what it is. In the Amazing Race, students get a bonus if they can also figure out what part of the world it originated in. The simple elimination of the recipe's title taps into the students' curiosity, and they approach the recipe so much differently not knowing what the outcome will be. It's a perfect example of how a small shift can make a big impact.

Variation for Science: Instead of teams following a recipe and trying to figure out what it is, they complete a lab experiment and try to guess what they've created. Or give a series of clues to teams that lead them to accurately guess the name of an animal, insect, plant, or planet, etc.

Variation for Social Studies: Teams are given clues to a certain event in history, and they have to guess the event within a certain amount of time. They receive bonus points if they guess the year.

Utensil Relay

In a utensil relay, teams race to quickly identify a kitchen utensil before anyone else by holding it up in the air. There are three rounds of play:

Round 1: I hold up a utensil.

Round 2: I say the name of the utensil.

Round 3: I say the use of the piece of utensil.

To start play, each team sends one person to their kitchen. I hold up a utensil and students hurriedly try to find that utensil in their kitchen and hold it in the air first. I give the team who found it first a point and then repeat two more times. Teams tap on another member, and the game play continues for three more utensils. When every member has gone once in Round 1, Round 2 begins. Teams with the most points by the end of Round 3 win.

This is a great game to play at the beginning of the school year to familiarize your students with the utensils and equipment within their kitchens.

Variation for Multiple Subject Areas: Divide your students into teams. Create sets of index cards with vocabulary terms or images from your content area and have each team spread them out into a grid in front of them. Play continues as above through each round, but instead of students finding the actual item, they hold up the index card with the matching term instead.

Minute to Win It

Based on the NBC television show, *Minute to Win It*, these are sixty-second challenges using household items that could be played in a variety of subject areas and grade levels. This is a great challenge to do at the beginning of the year as a team builder or as a brain break or opener to hook kids and get them excited about what's to come. There are endless possible ideas for sixty-second challenges, but here are a few to get you thinking. Think about others that may even tie into your content area.

- **Face the Cookie.** Pick one person from each team. Have them place a Nilla Wafer on their forehead and have them try to get it into their mouth without touching it with their hands within sixty seconds.
- **Suck It Up.** In this game, students transfer Smarties from one plate to another using only a straw within sixty seconds. The number of Smarties to transfer could vary depending on the age of the student playing.

- **Ping Pong.** In this game, students are given ten ping pong balls and have sixty seconds to bounce them into each of the ten cups.
- **Dicey.** A student places a spoon or popsicle stick in his or her mouth. Another team member balances six dice on the end by stacking them on each other within sixty seconds.
- **Breakfast Scramble.** Students reassemble the front of a cereal box that has been cut into sixteen even pieces within sixty seconds.

Cutthroat Kitchen

One of my favorite sources of inspiration is the Food Network television show, *Cutthroat Kitchen*. This cooking show, hosted by Alton Brown, features four chefs that compete in a three-round elimination cooking competition. At the start of the show, each chef is given $25,000. In each round, chefs have the opportunity to bid on auction items to sabotage one another. The person left standing at the end of the competition keeps whatever money he or she has not spent in the auctions.

My classroom version may be a little less cutthroat but equally as fun! At the start of the game, teams of three or four are given $1,000 of play money and a recipe to create. When the timer starts, each team will have one minute to collect ingredients needed from the supply table and bring them back to their kitchen. Any team not back in their kitchen by the timer "buzz" has one ingredient confiscated from their basket. Once all are back in their kitchens, the timer starts again, and teams begin to prepare the recipe and have it plated within the time allocated. At timed intervals throughout the challenge, I auction off various items that chefs can use to sabotage one another. This could include ingredient/equipment changes, restrictions (e.g., no talking, or one team member's hand must remain on his or her head), and loss of cooking time. The highest-bidding team pays for the item out of their $1,000 and decides which team will face the sabotage. When time ends, all sabotages are lifted, and teams bring their dishes to the judging panel and describe and explain their dish. The judges evaluate their dishes based on taste, presentation, and how closely it resembles the assigned dish on a provided rubric. The top three teams with the highest overall score are awarded money in increments of $1,000, $750, and $500. Teams add up their total money remaining, and those with the most money win the challenge. Students love this challenge! Friendly sabotage is always a favorite among students and creates a fun and immersive experience that keeps them guessing from beginning to end!

Variation for Multiple Subjects: Divide class into teams and give each a box or bag full of dried spaghetti, marshmallows, masking tape, and string. Instead of preparing a recipe, in this variation, the goal is to build the highest free-standing structure. Play continues as above until time runs out, auctioning off items to prevent the other teams from building the tallest structure. Teams with the tallest tower at the end win. Some of you may be thinking this sounds a lot like another challenge that many are familiar with: the Marshmallow Challenge. Exactly! When you take mechanics from various games that you know and morph them together to make your own, the results can be magical!

Turn on the television and do a little reality television binge watching. You'll be amazed at how many game mechanics you will pick up that you will be able to incorporate into your classes immediately! Adding a little challenge will take students' creativity, communication, critical thinking, and collaboration to new heights, and they will have so much fun; they won't even realize they are learning!

Let's Play!

Now that you have an overview of gamification, let's get specific. What follows are the games I've created for my classes and exactly how they are played. Each one is layered over one semester of content.

MASTERCHEF

Goal: Students are on a quest each unit to become MasterChef by earning 4,000 XP. They earn a Michelin Star each time they earn MasterChef status. The ultimate goal is to earn three Michelin Stars before the end of the semester.

Story

Theme: MasterChef

Setting: My room is transformed into the MasterChef kitchen.

Character: Students are aspiring chefs on a mission to acquire new culinary skills and earn three Michelin Stars by the end of the semester.

Action: Students participate in Mystery Box Challenges, Mini Games, and our MasterChef Challenge at the end of the unit. I break down each in more detail as I explain my game mechanics.

Game Mechanics

Experience Points and Badges

Students have an opportunity to earn tangible badges for demonstrating their learning in various ways throughout the unit. The badges hold various amounts of XP in increments of 250 XP and are collected to reach certain levels in the game. Students can earn them through extraordinary product quality in culinary labs, missions, mini challenges, mini games, and MasterChef Challenges. Creating a variety of opportunities to earn badges allows all learners to demonstrate their knowledge and skills in a way that they choose, which gives them autonomy and ownership in the game.

Levels

As students earn badges for demonstrating their learning, they accumulate experience points to reach levels leading up to MasterChef status. Throughout each unit, my students work toward becoming MasterChefs by earning 4,000 XP. When students reach MasterChef status, they have demonstrated an understanding of the content at such a level that they have earned mastery in our standards-based system for the learning target being assessed. Reaching this level isn't easy to do, but if reached, it has some awesome rewards. Because they have demonstrated their understanding of the content at a mastery level, they are exempt from taking the test. Not only that, but they get to have a free cooking day when everyone else is taking the test; additionally, when students earn MasterChef status, they are given a button with a Michelin Star and an apron to wear for the upcoming unit that is a different color from everyone else's. If students earn three Michelin Star buttons throughout the semester, they get an apron embroidered with their name on it to keep as well as their picture on the legacy wall. That is a big deal to my students! I have discovered that students who earn MasterChef status not only have earned their mastery grade, they have also exceeded it and truly have left a legacy in our classroom.

Although MasterChef status is the ultimate goal, there are other levels leading up to MasterChef status that students can achieve. If they earn 1,000 XP, they become Line Cook and are able to use an index card with their notes on the test, 2,000 XP earns them Sous Chef status, and they can either partner with another Sous Chef to take the test or use one page of notes. The various levels keep students motivated even if they don't feel they will earn MasterChef status.

The experience points reboot after each unit, which allows students a chance to start fresh.

Mystery Box Challenges

This challenge is an adaptation of one I learned from reality television food shows, and it is so much fun! I place an assortment of ingredients on a table with cloth covering it. Once the covering is removed, students have sixty minutes to prepare a dish using the ingredients available. Each challenge has slightly different rules and guidelines, and it is impressive to see students collaborate to create their dishes within a short amount of time.

Product Quality

Teams that have extraordinary product quality in the completion of every lab can earn a badge worth 500XP. Sometimes one team earns the badge, and sometimes a badge is earned by multiple teams. I am often the one evaluating the products, but sometimes I will have my Sous Chefs (student aides) or former MasterChefs from previous semesters evaluate as well.

Chance Cards

Chance Cards are put into a box, and when I notice students demonstrating extraordinary employability skills, I allow them to randomly grab a card from the box. It could be a student showing incredible initiative, empathy, resilience, drive, leadership, or any other skills you reinforce in your class.

Students can also trade their XP in for Chance Cards. If students reach a certain level at the end of a unit and have XP left over, they can trade every 500 XP in for a Chance Card; for instance, if a student reaches 2,000 XP to become a Sous Chef and has an additional

1,000 XP remaining, he or she would be able to redeem them for two Chance Cards. They love it! I have found that the students who may not be motivated as much by earning levels and becoming MasterChef absolutely love to earn the Chance Cards! I have even found some students who would prefer to turn all of their XP for Chance Cards. I once had a student who achieved MasterChef status almost every unit but preferred to take the test and turn in all of his XP for Chance Cards (eight altogether!) I hadn't anticipated this happening, but why not? Let the kids help design their learning experience! After all, they are the ones playing the game! Why not make it amazing for them?

Bakery Missions

Bakery Missions give students an opportunity to demonstrate their understanding of the content—above and beyond what they do in class. Missions are always related to the essential questions of the unit, are never given a grade, and always have an expiration date.

MasterChef Challenges

At the end of each unit, I take an essential skill that they learned and ask them to demonstrate it without a recipe and make it something delicious. In our pastry unit, I give students a formula for a pie crust that is missing the recipe instructions. I then challenge them to prepare the dough as a team and make it into something that will blow my mind! It can be something they have made before or something completely unique. The best part is that they are preparing this for a panel of judges. Teams that earn the highest scores win experience points: third place, 500 XP; 2nd place, 750 XP; and first place, 1,000 XP. (For more on the MasterChef Challenge, see page 54.)

Mini Games

At the end of each unit, I give students one final opportunity to earn experience points before they take the test. We have played Kahoot!, Quizlet Live, Quizizz, Quizalize, Gimkit, Mystery Box, and various other games that I have learned from other educators or have created myself. After the review game, I call students up to redeem their badges earned from the unit to determine what level they've achieved and let them know how to prepare for the test. If students have remaining XP (i.e., 500 XP over a level earned), they can trade every 500 XP in for a Chance Card to use throughout the remainder of the semester. I have even had students opt out of using notes and turning in all of their XP for Chance Cards. I have found that this option gives students some agency in the game and allows them to strategize. Refer to page 54 for the MasterChef Game Plan.

THE AMAZING FOOD TRUCK RACE

My MasterChef game was such a smashing success; I couldn't wait to gamify my other classes as well, but I knew the game design would need to be different due to the difference in content and class structure. Culinary 3 students learn about American Regional cuisine for the first semester. Inspired by the Food Network reality television show, *The Great Food Truck Race*, I began thinking about how I could adapt this theme to learn about the flavor profiles and cuisines of different United States regions.

In the television show, food truck teams race from the west coast to the east coast cooking, selling, and adapting to various challenges in the hopes of winning $50,000. Seed money is given to each truck at the beginning of each episode that can be used for grocery shopping. Every week the food truck teams face challenges to earn more money and experience obstacles that make the game more difficult. I loved this reality show's concept and thought it would be an awesome theme to layer over our semester-long American Regional Cuisine unit.

Goal: Food truck teams are on a race across the United States from Medford, Oregon, to Medford, Maine, learning about the flavor profiles and dishes that make up American Regional cuisine. At each stop, they have an opportunity to earn money from their regional challenge. The team that reaches Medford, Maine, with the most money wins the game!

Story

Theme: *The Great Food Truck Race*

Setting: Our classroom kitchens become food trucks that are traveling across the regions of the United States discovering America's best cuisine.

Characters: Our students become teams of food truck owners trekking across the United States to discover regional cuisine. When we launch the race, we invite staff and local chefs in as investors that provide students with seed money to start them on their journey across the United States. In each region we visit, staff and local chefs are invited back as customers who try the teams' signature dishes and award money to the highest-scoring teams.

Action: The action begins at the start of the game with the game launch and continues throughout each leg of the race with speed bump, truck stop, and regional challenges.

Game Mechanics

Food Truck Launch: To start the game, teams of three or four students create a food truck name, concept, and signature dish that they will adapt as they travel across the United States. We have a Food Truck Launch in my classroom where students come prepared with a commercial, sales pitch, plated menu item, and samples that they serve to an authentic audience of staff and local food truck owners.

The investors are given $2,000 of play money and a rubric to evaluate their presentation and menu item. Once all teams have presented, the investors divide up the money among the teams that they found most deserving.

Mini Challenges: In each region we visit, students face two different types of mini challenges:

- **Speed Bump Challenge:** In this challenge, students choose from a variety of regional flavors and ingredients that are placed on a cart. Students have sixty minutes to create something with the ingredients provided and present it to me and a panel of Culinary 4 student judges. Teams with the highest scores will be given grocery money in increments of $10, $5, and $2.50 for first, second, and third place. This money can be used on their signature dishes that are created for each regional challenge. Any money left over can be carried over into the next region.
- **Truck Stop Challenge:** In this challenge, students prepare a dish that originated in that region within a certain time period and present it to a panel of Culinary 4 judges and me. To add a special twist, sometimes students will have to unlock a series of clues on a Google form to reveal the dish that they will be making. As in the Speed Bump Challenge, teams with the highest scores will be given grocery money in increments of $10, $5, and $2.50 for first, second, and third place. This money can be used on their signature dishes that are created for each regional challenge as well. Any money left over can be carried over into the next region.

Regional Challenges: Food truck teams research and become experts on each region that we visit. They create a presentation explaining the region's flavor profiles, cuisine, and culture as well as adapt their signature dish to the flavor profiles and cuisine of that region. An authentic audience of staff and local chefs come in for the challenge and evaluate the teams' presentations and signature dishes. Top teams will earn money in increments of $2,000, $1,500, and $1,000. This money will be added to their running total as they race across America.

Grocery Money: Food truck teams have an opportunity to earn grocery money for each Speed Bump and Truck Stop Challenge. This money is used to purchase ingredients for their regional challenges.

Food Truck Earnings: Money is earned by teams during their regional challenges. This money is accumulated as they race across America. The team with the most money at the end wins!

Chance Cards: Students can earn Chance Cards for demonstrating amazing employability skills throughout the race as well as during mini challenges. They include incentives such as coupons reducing the cost of a grocery item, getting a head start in a challenge, or getting an extra point added to a mini challenge score. The Chance Cards are kept in a box and drawn at random.

As you can see, the structure of this game is completely different than my MasterChef game. That is the beauty of gamification. There is not a "one size fits all" approach. Each game design is personalized to your teaching style, passion, content, grade level, and goal. Remember, start small and go from there. Your game will evolve over time as you find what works best for your class and students.

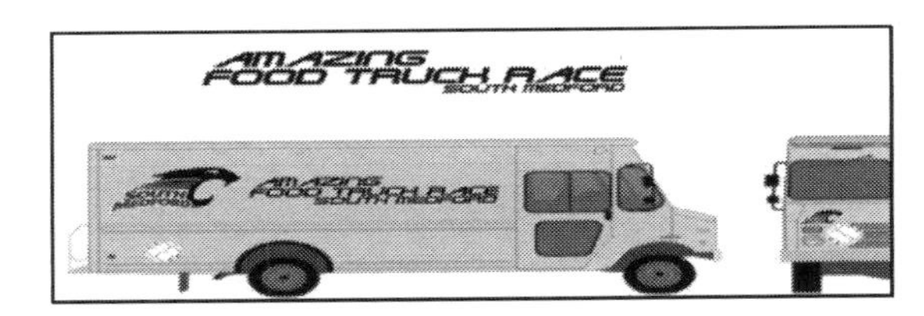

STORY

SETTING: Our classroom kitchens become food trucks that are traveling across the regions of the United States discovering America's best cuisine.

CHARACTER: Our students become teams of food truck owners trekking across the United States to discover regional cuisine.

ACTION: The action begins at the start of the game with the game launch and continues throughout each leg of the race with speed bump, truck stop, and regional challenges.

GOAL

Food truck teams are on a race across the United States from Medford, Oregon, to Medford, Maine, learning about the flavor profiles and dishes that make up American Regional cuisine. Each stop they have an opportunity to earn money from their regional challenge. The team that reaches Medford, Maine, with the most money wins the game!

REGIONS: ***NORTHWEST***
SOUTHWEST
MIDWEST
SOUTH
NORTHEAST

GAME MECHANICS

SPEED BUMP

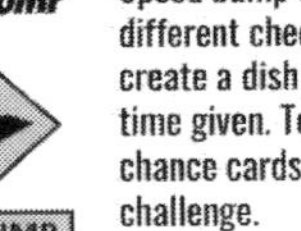

Speed bump challenges will be randomly issued at different checkpoints throughout the race. Teams will create a dish using regional ingredients within the time given. Teams with highest scores will earn chance cards and grocery items to use in the regional challenge.

TRUCK STOP

A roadblock is a mystery recipe that is to be prepared within the time frame given. Teams with the best overall quality will earn miles and grocery items to use in the pitstop challenge at the end of each leg. Bonus will be given to teams that discover recipe name and place of origin before time runs out.

REGIONAL CHALLENGES

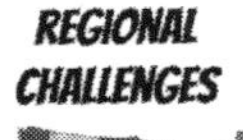

There will be a pitstop at the end of each leg of the race where you will share a dish and what you know about your teams selected country to an audience of customers. This is your time to shine!

THE AMAZING RACE

The structure of this next game is similar to *The Great Food Truck Race* but different enough that it changes things up and keeps the game fresh and exciting as we start a new semester. My inspiration for my theme is the reality television game show, *The Amazing Race,* that has been airing for thirty seasons on CBS. In this show, teams of two race around the globe competing with other contestants to get to each destination "Pit Stop" first. Contestants arriving first get special prizes and game advantages, and the last duo to arrive is eliminated from the race. As teams travel to various locations around the world, they unlock the clues provided at route markers in each leg that lead them to the next destination. Some clues direct them to perform a task that is related in some manner to the country wherein they are located or its culture. In each leg, teams are eliminated until three remain and vie to reach the final destination first.

I used the basic game structure and mechanics of this popular television show to create my own culinary version. This is my basic game plan; however, there are sure to be plenty of surprises along the way in our Amazing Race adventures!

Goal: Teams will embark on a race around the globe to explore flavors, culinary techniques, and meal-related customs. There will be four legs:

Leg 1: Europe

Leg 2: Mediterranean

Leg 3: Asia

Leg 4: Africa

The goal is to earn the most miles for your team and arrive at the final Pit Stop before the other teams.

Story

Theme: *The Amazing Race*

Setting: Our classroom is transformed into restaurants in various parts of the world as we "travel" around the globe and experience international cuisine.

Characters: Our students become teams of chefs trekking across the world to discover international cuisine. Staff and local chefs are invited in as judges for the Pit Stop challenge at the end of each leg of the race.

Action: To launch the game, teams of three or four students create a team name, logo, and video trailer that they will use to promote their team throughout the race. (I explain this in more detail later in this chapter.) Throughout each leg of the race, there are Detour and Road Block challenges that lead to a final Pit Stop challenge at the end of each leg.

Game Mechanics

Mini Challenges: In each region we visit, there are two different types of mini challenges:

- **Detours:** Detours will be randomly issued at different checkpoints throughout the race. Each detour gives teams the choice between two options to complete. Teams successfully completing detours earn miles and grocery item upgrades to use in the Pit Stop at the end of each leg.
- **Road Blocks:** A Road Block is a mystery recipe to be prepared within the time frame given. Teams with the best overall quality will earn miles and grocery items to use in the Pit Stop Challenge at the end of each leg. A bonus will be given to teams who discover recipe name and place of origin before time runs out.

Fast-Forwards: Fast-Forwards are a series of clues to unlock within each leg of the race. Unlocking the clues will give you first choice of countries to research for the upcoming leg and other surprises and perks as well.

Pit Stop: There will be a Pit Stop at the end of each leg of the race where teams will share a dish and their research of their selected country to an audience of customers. Teams with the highest score from the customers will earn miles in the race.

Grocery Upgrades: Teams have an opportunity to earn grocery upgrades for each Detour and Road Block they face in the race legs. Upgrades allow students to build on basic items that they get for their recipes at each Pit Stop. The upgrades are in the form of laminated Chance Cards that are put in a box and drawn at random. Some examples of Upgrade cards include Produce Upgrade, Protein Upgrade, Dairy Upgrade, Mix-in Ingredient, Double Your Protein, and Double Your Mix-in. Sabotage cards can give teams an advantage by allowing them to take an item of choice from another team. Block cards allow the team being sabotaged to block the item from being taken, and Boomerangs bounce the sabotage back to the team who is issuing it.

Miles: Miles are earned by teams for Detours, Road Blocks, and Pit Stop Challenges. These miles accrue as they race across the world. The team with the most miles at the end wins.

The beauty of gamification is that there is no end to the possibilities. There is not a "one size fits all" approach. Each game design is personalized to your teaching style, passion, content, grade level, and goal. Remember, start small and go from there. Your game will evolve over time as you find what works best for your class and students.

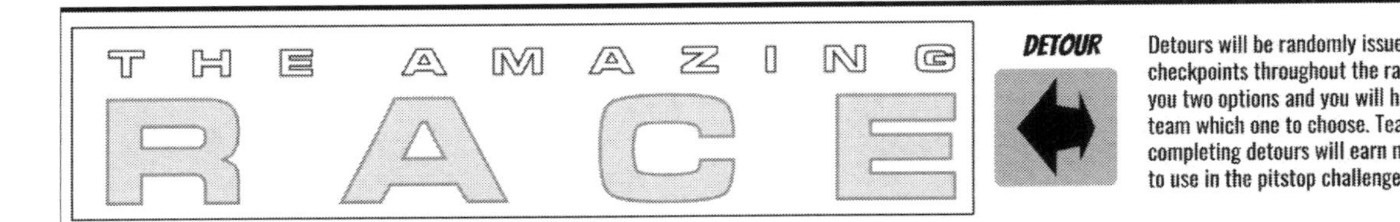

STORY

SETTING: Our classroom is transformed into restaurants in various parts of the world as we "travel" around the global and experience international cuisine.

CHARACTER: Our students become teams of chefs trekking across the world to discover international cuisine. Staff and local chefs are invited in as judges for the pitstop challenge at the end of each leg of the race.

ACTION: The action begins at the start of the game with the game launch and continues throughout each leg of the race with Detour and Road Block challenges that lead to a final Pitstop challenge at the end of each leg.

GOAL

Teams embark on a race around the globe to explore flavors, culinary techniques, and meal related customs.

There are four legs of the race:

Leg 1: Europe
Leg 2: Mediterranean
Leg 3: Asia
Leg 4: Africa

The goal is to earn the most miles for your team and arrive at the final Pitstop before the other teams.

DETOUR

Detours will be randomly issued at different checkpoints throughout the race. Each detour will give you two options and you will have to determine as a team which one to choose. Teams successfully completing detours will earn miles and grocery items to use in the pitstop challenge at the end of each leg.

ROAD BLOCK

a road block is a mystery recipe that is to be prepared within the time frame given. Teams with the best overall quality will earn miles and grocery items to use in the pitstop challenge at the end of each leg. Bonus will be given to teams that discover recipe name and place of origin before time runs out.

FAST FORWARD

Fast forwards are a series of clues to unlock within each leg of the race. Unlocking the clues will give you first choice of countries to research for the upcoming leg and other surprise perks as well.

PITSTOP

There will be a pitstop at the end of each leg of the race where you will share a dish and what you know about your teams selected country to an audience of customers. This is your time to shine!

Game Launch

If you truly want to get students excited about your gamified class, you can't just begin; you must have an explosive launch! Each game launch in my classroom begins with a video trailer that builds anticipation, excitement, and intrigue as to what's to come. Like a movie trailer, it gives just enough information to hook the viewer while still leaving a little curiosity. To give you a little taste of what this looks like in my classroom, I will explain my launch into International Cuisine for The Amazing Race:

On game day, students come in to *The Amazing Race* theme song playing in the background. Eight tables are set up, each with a Chromebook and an envelope labeled "Route Information." Projected on the screen are the words "Get ready! The first leg of The Amazing Race is about to begin!"

I play the promotional trailers the students have created to get them fired up and then have them stand behind their team table. I tell students that when the clock starts, they are on a race to find their first route marker. They need to open the envelope, which contains three images, and figure out what location they all have in common. Once they determine that location, which is Lyon, France, they must run to find it on the globe I have at the front of the room. If they guess correctly, they will be handed another envelope that contains another clue. This clue is an image of a famous restaurant in Lyon. They have to locate the image in Google Maps, and in Street View, find the man in the red chef's coat. This man holds the first route marker! When teams show me the man in red, I hand them a laminated route marker that is numbered with the place in which they arrived (i.e., first, second, third, etc.).

Selecting Countries

Once all teams have received their route markers, it is time to select their countries. The first leg of the race is in Europe, and students can choose from one of four countries that I have chosen. Teams then select the country that they will research and prepare a local dish. Students have four weeks before they arrive at the Pit Stop, where they will present what they've learned and the dish they prepared from that country to an authentic audience of chefs and staff members.

The name of each country is on an index card with the word "entree" or "dessert." To keep things exciting, I also write "Wild Card" on one card, and if a team chooses the "Wild Card," they can select anywhere in Europe that they'd like. Starting with the Route Marker #1, teams in consecutive order select their country and meal category for the first leg of the race.

The level of positive energy in the room during game launch day is always electric! I could have just told them where we were going at the start of the class period and assigned countries to each team, but it wouldn't have been nearly as much fun. I guarantee you the energy would not have been nearly as high. It took a little time to plan, but I had a blast doing it. It's so much fun creating experiences that you know your students are going to love. As Dave Burgess says, "Provide an uncommon experience for your students, and they will reward you with an uncommon effort and attitude."

Teaming Up

On launch day, I show the promotional video trailer, which leads directly into students forming teams, creating names, and producing their own promotional video trailers. Spending a few days doing this allows students to bond with new team members before the race begins. I love the laughter, fun, and creativity that goes into the creation of each of the team names and their video productions.

On the Fly

Some days you feel like all the stars have aligned, and a sprinkling of pixie dust landed on your classroom because everything goes just as planned. Those days are magical! Then there are those "not so magical days." You know, the days where nothing quite goes as planned. You keep pouring cup after cup of coffee thinking you may just need a little more caffeine.

One of my greatest successes came on one of those "not so magical days." One mishap had turned into another mishap, and no matter how hard I tried to recover, the mishaps kept coming. I should have known when I began my fourth-period class that it wasn't likely things would go as planned. Sure enough, they didn't. I had planned an amazing classroom escape room activity orchestrated perfectly with iPads ready to scan the QR code that would bring them to the digital escape room. I had tested them, and everything was good to go. When students came in, I hyped up the game, and they were all champing at the bit to team up for this challenge. I started the timer, and off they went—until they scanned the QR code to find out the Wi-Fi was down. Yep. None of the iPads connected, and the escape room activity couldn't be accessed. To make matters worse, my sophomore son was in this class. He looked at me with his big brown eyes, and I immediately knew what he was thinking: *How is she going to recover from this? I really don't want to see her fail. My reputation is on the line here.*

That's when my teacher-mama powers went into overdrive. I had to find a solution on the fly. I glanced at my counter and saw the game Code Names and remembered an idea that I had tried at a workshop I facilitated but hadn't yet tried with my students. As I began to give instructions, I was literally formulating a plan in my brain: "Class, we are going to create a game called Culinary Code Names." Did I know this was going to work? Absolutely not. But I was going to give it my best shot.

It worked, and the students loved it—including my son! I adapted the original Code Names game to match my content, and you can too! Think about how you could change the player titles, card names, and game scenario to match your content.

CULINARY CODE NAMES

Game Scenario

Two restaurants have been temporarily shut down due to a failed restaurant inspection. The Executive Chefs are on a race against the clock to find the source of the failed score and save their restaurant from closing forever.

Materials Needed

- Two hundred index cards cut in half
- The map cards from the original Code Names game
- Plastic stand from original game (You can buy extras on Amazon.)
- Blue, red, and white tokens or card stock cut into blue, red, and white squares
- One black poker chip or card stock cut into a square

Rules

1. Divide class into teams of three or four students.
2. Pair teams up so two teams are playing against one another: one red team and one blue team.

3. Select one player from each team to be the Executive Chef (Spymaster in original game); all other team members will be employees.
4. Pass out the following to each team:
    - Twenty-five index card halves
    - Nine red, blue, and white tokens or squares
    - One black token or square
    - Three Code Name Map cards (from original game)
    - A pen
5. Have each team come up with fifty culinary words to write on the front and back of each index card. Words can be ingredients, utensils, equipment, or cooking terms. If you teach another subject, you could have them write vocabulary words/terms that relate to your content.

Tomato

6. Teams will set out cards randomly in a five-by-five grid, so all line up in straight rows.
7. The Executive Chefs from each team will be given a map card that identifies the cards that are on the grid. The red and blue

spaces identify the supplies that belong to each team. The tan spaces are neutral spaces, and the black spaces identify the contaminated card. Use the small plastic stand to keep the map card upright for only the Executive Chefs to see.

8. Each map card has four small rectangles, one on each side of the map grid, that indicate which team plays first. The team that plays first has one more supply to uncover than the other team.
9. The Executive Chefs will take turns trying to get their team to find their supplies before the other team finds theirs. Each will call out a one-word hint to describe the supplies that they are trying to get their team to identify, followed by the number of cards the hint relates to.
10. Line cooks must make at least one guess after the Chef gives the hint. If they guess the card(s) correctly, the Chef covers it with a token of their team color. If it is wrong, it must be covered by the token that it belongs to according to the map card. If they pick the contaminated card, the game is immediately over, and the guessing team loses.
11. The game ends when a team wins by guessing all of their supplies on the grid or loses by guessing the contaminated card.

What is your favorite game? Apples to Apples, Jeopardy, Catan? How could you take games that you love and adapt them to your content? Open up that game cabinet and let your mind run wild! The possibilities are only limited to your imagination!

So Much More Than Fun and Games

There is something magical about my family cabin in winter. There are no agendas, "to do" lists, or alarm clocks. The way the snow sparkles, the snow birds that peak in through our window, and the cozy fireplace all make for the perfect retreat; however, what I love best is how our family comes together around the dining room table for game play. Hours upon hours are spent around our table playing family favorites: Hearts, Dominoes, Progressive Rummy, Hand and Foot, Cribbage, and Dutch Blitz. I truly savor this time for so many reasons.

Since gamifying my classroom, I have gained a new appreciation for my favorite family pastime. I love the playful fun that games bring: the smiles, laughter, and excitement. I have found this dynamic to be true in the gamified classroom as well. When students are having a good time learning, the energy is electric, and they are fully immersed; however, let me assure you that games and gamification done right extends far beyond that. The challenge, collaboration, creativity, and critical thinking that are woven into game play bring a complexity that goes much deeper than points and badges.

Challenge

My kids were reintroduced to some card games this weekend that they hadn't played in a long time. As I watched them struggle to learn the game mechanics and rules at the beginning, I thought about it through the eyes of an educator. There was frustration and failure, but my kids were challenged. They were not motivated by the rules but by how to develop their own strategies to master the skills. As my daughter reflected on the card game "Hearts" tonight, she said, "I am excited to play tomorrow because now that I understand the rules, I have some new ideas of how I can strategize." Isn't this what we want for our students? We want them to be challenged to persevere through the struggle and failure and motivated to develop their own strategies to attain mastery.

Collaboration

Something special happens when we gather the family around the table with a game. The laughter and excitement that games bring bonds us in a special way. Everyone is completely immersed as they are collaborating and communicating on how to win the game. Let's think about this dynamic in our classrooms. Creating a sense of community is so vital to building a classroom where learning thrives. Don't we want students to laugh and be excited about learning? What would learning look like if students were continually collaborating and communicating about how to master the content? How would it change the culture to have students who supported and celebrated one another's accomplishments?

Creativity

The game Snake Oil has become a new family favorite. In this game, players have to sell an item to "the customer" by selecting two cards in their hands to combine together. The players have to be creative with their sales pitch, thinking about why the customer would benefit from the item they are selling. The game is hilarious because players are required to think on their feet and come up with convincing arguments with very little time to think through what they are going to say. I love the creativity that comes out when players are challenged to do so in a short amount of time. I have noticed this same dynamic happen in my classroom. When students are challenged to take their skills and demonstrate their learning in a creative way, they blow my mind. Sometimes we put too many parameters on student learning. Give students challenging opportunities to be creative and watch them soar!

Critical Thinking

Reflecting on all of the various mechanics in the games we play as a family makes me realize how much critical thinking was required. Let me use the card game Hearts as an example. In this game, players strategically play their cards to avoid collecting Hearts and the Queen of Spades. You are continually thinking critically about what move you are going to make next so you can end the game with the fewest points possible. In the gamified classroom, students are also critically thinking about the content. In culinary, they are daily analyzing, evaluating, interpreting, and synthesizing the content and creatively thinking about how they are going to solve problems that arise. Students are not merely consumers of information; they are learning by doing, empowered to create their own learning adventure.

I am grateful for the time of laughter and fun and the memories made around the game table. I know that translates to the classroom as well, and the magic truly happens where students are immersed in a rich learning environment full of challenge, collaboration, creativity, and critical thinking.

Gamify Your Classroom for a Magical Experience

There are so many ways to bring games into your classroom. Clearly, my favorite approach is to make the entire class or course a game. Remember that you can take small steps toward gamification and, in the meantime, have a whole lot of fun—and provide some magical learning opportunities.

- What is your favorite game to play? What do you enjoy about it?
- How could you adapt elements from that game into your course, unit, or even a single lesson?
- What is your favorite television reality or game show? How could you use challenges from it to create fun and educational experiences for your students?
- What preconceptions or reservations have you had about gamification? What in this chapter has challenged you to consider this approach to learning?

For more information about how to gamify your classroom, check out this resource from Michael Matera, author of *Explore Like a Pirate!*

Chapter 5
Innovation

Everywhere I turn, I find frustrated teachers. These words echo in my head from bits of conversations I hear on a regular basis:

Kids today . . .
want to be entertained.
don't show up on time.
are entitled.
lack focus.
are lazy.
don't meet deadlines.
I'm stressed because there is/are . . .
so much pressure.
too many initiatives.
too many students.
too many hoops.
not enough time.

Sound familiar?

Some weeks it takes everything in me to fight these thoughts from taking root in my mind. Just like you, I get exhausted, frustrated, and overwhelmed. During one particularly stressful week mid-semester, I worked to push those negative thoughts back by taking some time to reflect on what I do and how I do it. The words "innovate inside of the box" came to mind, so I picked up one of my favorite books, *The Innovator's Mindset,* by George Couros and began reading . . .

Let's not kid ourselves. In education, especially the public sector, schools are not overloaded with funding. Innovating in our schools requires a different type of thinking, one that doesn't focus on ideas that are "outside of the box" but those that allow us to be innovative despite budgetary constraints. In other words, we need to learn to innovate inside the box.

Many of us in education can say our schools are lacking either funding, resources, time, technology, or support. It's the box we live in; however, it's how we innovate inside those constraints that makes the difference. Do we focus on all the limitations we have, or do we get creative and think about how we can do something new and better within the box we are given? Innovation—thinking about things differently, shaking up the status quo, and devising new and better ways of teaching—is how we make learning magical. To get there, we have to have the mindset of an innovator.

George describes eight characteristics of an innovator's mindset in his book. And while I've not mastered these characteristics perfectly, I know that being aware of them and intentionally working to develop them has helped to shift my mindset in the past few years. I want to share them with you because I know these traits have saved me from the frustrations and burnout that so many educators face, and I know they can help you too.

1. **Empathetic**—I regularly ask myself the question George poses: "Would I want to be a learner in my own classroom?" We can't expect our students to respond to the same methods of learning that we did. They are growing up in a different era. When we put ourselves in their shoes and see the world as they do, we will create learning experiences that are powerful. Inspired by Tara Martin's #BookSnaps idea, my students create #FoodSnaps to reflect on their creations using Snapchat, a tool that speaks their language. This is just one example of finding ways to create learning experiences that meet students where they are.
2. **Problem Finders/Solvers**—I spend a lot less time on posing problems to students and let them find the problems instead. So much learning happens when we get out of the way and encourage our students to find their own solutions. They become empowered and truly make learning their own. Instead of feeding students tons of information to consume, my goal is to have students find the information on their own as well as find and solve their own problems. To take their learning further, I create authentic audiences by inviting in restaurant owners and staff for students to share their learning with. This takes the learning experience to a completely different level as the relevance and meaning skyrockets.
3. **Risk Takers**—For many years, I waited for perfection before I launched a new idea or lesson. The reality was, more often than not, perfection never came, and I just maintained the status quo in fear that my new idea would fail. Since embracing an innovator's mindset, I don't fear risk-taking anymore. I am continually pushing the boundaries of what's possible to create amazing experiences for my students. Those ideas and lessons do fail at times, but the wins far outweigh the

losses, and I've grown leaps and bounds in the iterative process of refining my practice. I also have found that modeling that risk-taking with my students is so vital. Students get used to my crazy ideas and embrace them as we learn together. Experiencing my boldness in teaching gives them the freedom to risk boldly too. So much growth happens when we take big leaps.

4. **Networked**—There was a time that I lived in a culinary silo. I went through my school days feeling isolated and alone. How could anyone relate to my world of chef's knives and sauté pans? I was so wrong. Once I discovered Twitter and began developing a PLN, a whole new world opened up to me! I realized that it was ridiculous to remain in a culinary silo when there were educators from across the educational spectrum, from kindergarten through higher education, whom I could learn from and collaborate with! I began to share the learning that was happening in my class and found ways to integrate the ideas I had gained from other educators into my class. I started participating in and even moderating Twitter chats to develop deeper connections. I joined in Voxer communities to discuss books and topics that I was passionate about. Without a doubt, I've grown exponentially as an educator since I've become globally connected.
5. **Observant**—George Couros says, "Sometimes the most valuable thing you get from the network isn't an idea but the inspiration or courage to try something new." I find this to be so true. I have become so much more courageous in my teaching as I've been inspired by my PLN. I look at my world through new lenses now as well. When I read, run, hike, watch television, people watch, and go through my normal day-to-day life, I am continually looking for inspiration to bring into

my classroom. So many ideas are just waiting for us to grab hold of them and make them our own brand of awesome!

6. **Creators**—Learning is powerful when students go beyond consumption to creation. My classes are creation-based by nature; students are collaborating on a daily basis to create amazing food. Creating takes on a whole new meaning when students don't simply follow recipes but instead use the skills and techniques they learn to make something entirely new. Empowering students to make learning their own and come up with their own creations is one of the most powerful things to experience as an educator. To see their faces light up with pride as they present their unique and delicious dishes makes my heart leap with joy. Learning becomes so much more rich and meaningful when we give students opportunities to create and connect at this level.
7. **Resilient**—Not long ago, my students reviewed safety and sanitation by working in teams to solve a classroom escape room activity. I have never seen my students so engaged and immersed in learning about safe food-handling practices during my seventh block of the day. The challenge was difficult, but they were all in—well, all but one student whose comment made me bristle: "Mrs. Richmond, why don't you just have us do a worksheet? It would be easier." *Well, yes it would be easier, much easier,* I thought.

   But easy isn't the point. Answers regurgitated on a worksheet would not be retained or hold as much meaning as what students learn through the critical thinking and collaborating that happens when students work together to unlock the series of digital escape room clues. How often are we encouraging our students to stretch their thinking? Are we feeding them the answers or challenging them in a safe environment where they can take risks, fail, and risk again?

I've come to realize that not everyone is going to agree with my approach to teaching and learning. It hurts sometimes, but I know what I'm doing works because my students are evidence of that. I have to continue doing what I know is working, even when others don't see the value or agree.

8. **Reflective**—One of the most powerful things I've begun to do as an educator is reflect regularly. Blog writing has become a wonderful and powerful way for me to not only document and share my learning but to also reflect on it myself. The more I do it, the more I crave it. I am able to make deeper connections as I put my practice into words and truly think about what is working and what is not. I also love to sketchnote my learning. When I read a book, attend a professional development session or conference, or listen to a podcast, I often sketch my learning during and after to make deeper connections and allow it to resonate. As George states, "Looking back is crucial to moving forward." Having my blog posts and sketchnotes to look back on has been powerful for me as I continue to learn and grow as an educator.

I can't express enough how powerful these innovator's mindset characteristics have been in my EDUjourney. They have helped transform me as an educator as I have embraced "change as an opportunity to do something amazing."

Teaching is extremely hard work. We invest so much of ourselves in the lives of kids. There are days I am frustrated, tired, and feel like I do not have an ounce of energy left. All that to say, since developing an innovator's mindset, those days don't define me as an educator. No matter how strong my feelings of frustration or exhaustion get, my passion for teaching and learning is stronger. Innovation is contagious! Don't get stuck in your box. Find ways to do something amazing within it. The more you innovate, the more you'll crave it!

The Problem with Practically Perfect

One of the tallest hurdles I faced as I embraced innovation was my need to be perfect. To quote Mary Poppins, I wanted to be "practically perfect in every way." Looking back now, I realize what a stumbling block perfection has been for me over the years. I love this magical nanny with the talking umbrella, but my need for perfection prevented me from learning and growing. A better phrase to embrace would be "practically passionate in every way." When I began to let go of the need to have perfectly scripted and tidy lessons and instead pursued passionate teaching and learning, my mindset shifted. I was able to see that I had unrealistic expectations for myself as a teacher that were resulting in maintaining the status quo.

When I first integrated iPads into my classroom, I was overwhelmed by all of the apps that were available. I had heard about so many amazing creation tools, and the thought that I had to learn them all paralyzed me. When I finally let go of the idea that I had to be the expert and empowered my students to become the experts instead, my room suddenly became a place of innovation and possibility. When we give students the opportunity to explore, we unleash creativity. Sometimes, just like us, they need a little nudge to make the first leap.

In my Culinary 3 class, students research American regional cuisine. In each unit, they are exploring the region's flavor profiles, cuisine, and culture and then creating a presentation and a dish to share with an authentic audience. I discovered quickly that, even though I allowed them to use any creation tool they wanted to demonstrate their learning, they chose familiar tools rather than learning something new. Even when I pointed out that there were many more options on their devices than iMovie and Google Slides, they feared venturing from those platforms. That lack of initiative to try something new frustrated me until I realized that they were experiencing the same "practically perfect" syndrome that plagued me. If I'm asked to complete a task within a certain amount of time, I'm going to go with what I know because I know what the result will be. Taking the time to learn a new tool isn't worth the additional mental energy for the opportunity to be creative when I am not certain that it will end with a "perfect" result. It's so easy to gravitate towards the comfortable and predictable rather than challenge ourselves to try something that could potentially be new and better.

By stepping into my students' shoes, I was able to think about how to encourage them to push past the comfortable and take a risk. They needed some time to play and explore, and they needed a little guidance to get started. With so many apps on our iPads, my students didn't even know where to begin. It was overwhelming for them. To ease the sense of trepidation, I wrote out all of the creation apps on slips of paper and threw them into a bowl. Students paired up and randomly chose an app out of the bowl to explore. I set the timer for fifteen minutes and challenged the students to learn how the app worked and think of how it could be used in their regional presentations. I then explained that after the fifteen minutes, each pair would mirror their iPads to the AppleTV and share their findings with the class. Giving students a structured time frame and direction on what to look for guided their exploration. As students shared their findings with the class, I could hear the excitement in their voices. Their discoveries had unlocked their creativity, and they were ready to try something new. In the conversations and collaboration that followed, students asked one another about the apps they had explored, and they began to discuss how they could combine some of the apps together to create an appsmash of creation tools.

The next set of presentations they created were off the charts. They shared their learning with increased energy and enthusiasm, and it was easy to see they felt more empowered than ever. Although the opportunity to be innovative had always been there, they needed a gentle nudge and some direction. Trying something new can be scary for anyone. As educators, we need to provide the safety and structure to help students take the leap to new learning.

It's also important to understand that you don't have to be an expert with the tools before you introduce them to your students. I certainly didn't know how to expertly use all of the apps my students investigated in those fifteen minutes. But as the students explored the apps on their own, they learned a lot, and they made discoveries about the tools' capabilities that I wouldn't have. In part, that's because they were learning about the tool and using it from the student perspective—which is sometimes different from the way that we look at tools. When students become the experts, they own it. By empowering our students with opportunities to explore, create, fail, and iterate, they grow as a result. Let's put ourselves in our students' shoes and provide them with the structure and support to innovate, then sit back and watch them soar.

Trust Your Journey

A few Christmases ago, a dear friend and colleague gave me a beautiful pin with the words "Trust Your Journey." The words brought tears to my eyes as I thought about the wild journey I'd been on those previous few years. I've experienced a myriad of emotions, bouncing from fear to courage then doubt to excitement, as I've taken risks that I never thought I would take. This quest, to find new and better ways to solve problems and better serve those I teach and lead by developing an innovator's mindset, has been a wild ride. I've developed friendships that have given me the encouragement and support when I've most needed it. I've uncovered passions, dreams, and truths about myself that had not yet been realized; I've become a truer version of me. As George Couros states, "Innovation is not about the stuff; it is a way of thinking. I no longer am satisfied with the status quo; I see 'change as an opportunity to do something amazing.'"

I will say that there have been days when the journey has terrified me beyond belief. I've had moments of irrational fear and doubt when I've strongly considered going back to comfortable and easy; however, the fire inside me is too strong. I know that I can never go back to comfortable and easy, because in the discomfort and challenge is where I've experienced such growth. In the fear, I've discovered things about myself I hadn't realized and become even more certain of what I believe and hold dear to my heart. I am more confident and sure of the message I want to share with the world. As I look at the journey ahead, I have so many amazing opportunities that are going to require me to jump high and far. The truth is, my excitement bounces to fear within an instant. I'm on a roller coaster ride of emotions from one day to the next. When I look back on the jumps I've made in the past few years, I realize that each one I took started with the same degree of fear. Without taking those jumps, I would not have realized my passions, those things that fuel me and give me purpose. Each jump opened up an opportunity for another, and now looking back, each one seems so much smaller than it did at the time. I'm going to jump far and high and trust my journey.

When My Brain Backfires

My very first car was handed down to me by my grandparents. Living out in the country, this beauty was my ticket to freedom. No longer would I be the first student on the bus in the morning or the last person off. I wouldn't be relying on my friends to drive out of their way on the long dirt road to pick me up. I loved that quirky car and how it opened up my world to new opportunities. One of its most memorable personality traits was its spontaneous way of backfiring at the most inopportune times. I'd press down on the gas pedal to accelerate, and after a good four-second pause, it would lurch forward with an explosive pop from the tailpipe. It made for a good laugh among friends and fond memories of a quirky car with an explosive personality.

There are days when I feel much like that Ford Fairmont of my youth. I press down on the accelerator ready for a burst of innovative inspiration . . . and nothing; instead, I get a flood of emotion and frustration because I have all this time, and I'm paralyzed. This is not abnormal for me. I've experienced it my entire life. My mind moves at a million miles per hour with ideas racing around at breakneck speeds. I yearn for moments of solitude when they can all settle down and place themselves in logical order. Then when those precious moments finally come, the ideas all pause in my brain, all jumbled up and just waiting to lurch forward. I used to get so incredibly frustrated by this. When I press down on my accelerator, I want my brain to respond immediately. I don't want to wait. The reality is, that's not how my brain works. The ideas will flow when they're ready, and they almost always come with an explosive pop eventually. So I've learned to embrace the solitude, accept the fact that the ideas aren't flowing, and relax because I know that when my brain backfires, it will eventually lurch forward and pop with an explosion of innovation. I just need to be patient.

Living in a Jetsons World

If you grew up in the 1970s, you will recognize "Meet George Jetson" as the beginning of a popular futuristic cartoon theme song from back in the day. You may even start singing along! *The Jetsons* was one of my favorite cartoons to watch on a Saturday morning. Watching the episodes today, I realize that many of those futuristic inventions from the cartoon are indeed part of our everyday life. The home computer, cell phone, microwave oven, treadmill, teleconferencing, and robotics have become essential to our existence in 2018.

Looking back on my childhood, my love for that futuristic cartoon may have been a good indicator that I would become increasingly passionate about innovation as I grew older. I've always enjoyed dreaming about the possibilities for creating something new and better. Dreaming is not enough for me; I want to make those dreams a reality. One step toward the Jetsons' lifestyle for me included purchasing an Echo Dot (on sale on Cyber Monday). My intention was to use it for playing music in the kitchen while I was making dinner and maybe to ask Alexa random questions. I got more than I bargained for.

On any given day, I walk into my kitchen and say, "Alexa, play James Taylor."

And Alexa answers, "Shuffling songs by James Taylor."

Within two seconds, my favorite song, "Fire and Rain," is playing. If the volume is a little low, I can ask Alexa to turn up the volume, and sure enough, the volume increases. It's like the Jetsons' world that I dreamed of when I was a little girl.

Pondering the power of this little round dot, I wondered what else Alexa could do. Of course, my mind went straight to the classroom. As an educator who is passionate about the power of play, I wondered if Alexa played games. Searching the app, I discovered that Alexa *loves* to play games—and offers endless games to choose from. The question then was how to narrow down the games and find the ones that I could use for student learning. Thinking of my International Cuisine course, I searched for "world trivia," and low and behold, 136 results showed up! Country Game, World Quiz, My World Capitals, and so many more. My heart raced as I realized the potential for this in my Culinary Arts 3 The Amazing Race gamified semester.

My mental wheels spun so fast that sparks started to fly! I had to discover what else Alexa could play. I searched "food trivia" and, sure enough, sixty-three results. Food facts, Food Trivia, Noodle It Out, Cuisine Trivia, and more. Holy *wow*! This was incredible! What about picking teams? Could Alexa roll a dice or spin a wheel? Yes, she can. Type in "dice," and you will find ninety-one results! Spin a wheel? Yep, she can do that too. I even discovered she can tell "punny food puns" or choose a flavor on a wheel!

Who knew that this little white dot named Alexa could bring a whole new world of experiences into my classroom? I still love that she can play music by my man, James Taylor, at a moment's notice, but she is capable of so much more! Tapping into that little circle of technology opened a treasure box of new things to try and discover.

Innovate with Magic in Mind

We live in a world that is changing at an unbelievable rate of speed. When we are open to using technology in innovative ways and adapting existing things for new purposes, we have the opportunity to make learning magical.

- What are some ways that you have innovated in your current educational role?
- How have you adapted an existing thing and repurposed it into something new and better?
- What are some ways you've used technology in innovative ways in your classroom or school?

Chapter 6

Creativity, Collaboration, and Curiosity

Imagining something may be the first step in making it happen, but it takes the real time and real efforts of real people to learn things, make things, turn thoughts into deeds or visions into inventions.

–Fred Rogers

The magic of a classroom that comes alive begins with the making. Making happens daily in my culinary classes. Although we don't always complete something in one class period, creation is almost always a part of the learning. When I teach new vocabulary, methods, or techniques, creating always follows. There is something about taking a new learned term and immediately applying it that cements it in students' minds. They are experiencing learning by interacting with the ingredients and the process in a tangible way, and all of their senses are involved.

Make It!

My favorite part of the creating process is how it empowers students to own their learning. As students make, they are building a variety of skills that they are able to draw from to personalize their learning. In my Culinary 2 classes, my favorite part of the creating happens at the end of the unit when they break free from the recipe. Students are challenged to draw from their knowledge of the skills learned in the unit to prepare a dish. They are only given a list of the ingredients and amounts but no recipe. They can do some research ahead of time, but on the day of the challenge, there is no technology or information to draw from. Not only am I asking them to prepare a dish without the recipe, I also tell them to create something of restaurant quality. This is often when I meet their gazes with a look of disbelief—*no recipe, and it has to be amazing*? But when I set them free to collaborate with their team, something magical happens. They realize they do know how to make this dish, and they don't need no stinkin' recipe to do it! They've learned the formula, methods, and skills involved, and now they get to sprinkle in their own pixie dust and make their own unique creations. Their confidence rises as their imaginations run wild with possibilities. They find freedom in being able to apply the skills they know, and they experience such pride in making something that is uniquely their own.

Your classes may not involve food, but each content area has its forms of recipes. Isn't a recipe a formula that is made with a method or series of steps? What recipes are you teaching your students, and how can you give them an opportunity to sprinkle in their own pixie dust to make them their own? Here are ideas from my classroom. How can you adapt them for your own?

Bakery Missions

Bakery Missions are opportunities for students to go above and beyond our classroom experiences to demonstrate their learning in unique ways. As I introduced in the gamification chapter, I launch one mission for each Essential Question in a unit. Here is an example:

BAKERY MISSION:
CAKE INGREDIENT FUNCTIONS

MISSION:
Explain the functions of each cake ingredient and how it affects cake quality.

INSTRUCTIONS:
Use technology to thoroughly explain each cake ingredient function and the effects of too much or too little in a recipe.

APP SMASH IDEAS:
Paper 53 + Thing Link
Camera Roll + Adobe Voice + Flipgrid
Paper 53 + Tellagami

BONUS:
Everyone who completes level 3 will get to draw out of the XP bowl for surprise bonus points!

LEVELS
Level 1: Google Doc + Visuals 500 XP
Level 2: App Smash 750 XP
Level 3: iMovie or green screen video 1000 XP

These missions are not graded or required; however, completing them will earn students experience points that will move them closer to becoming a MasterChef. Not every kid will decide to accept the mission, but the advantages to earning experience points will benefit them later in the unit. To "launch" them, I share the mission as a Google Classroom assignment. Of course, special music adds a bit of drama as the mission is announced. I try to create a variety within each mission to allow for different interests, learning styles, and accessibility. The missions are something that go above and beyond the classroom learning, so I don't carve out class time for this. Students can complete them at home, during office hours, or before or after school in my class if I'm available. Once in a while, if students get done early with a class activity, I'll give them the extra time to work on it as well. I love how these bakery missions allow students to unleash their creativity and personalize their learning. Often students' completed missions are then shared to help others study for upcoming tests as an additional resource.

The possibilities for missions are endless. I try to keep them fairly open-ended to allow for students to truly add their own creative learning style. They can be as tech or non-tech as you want them to be.

Mission Recipe

1 cup Creativity

1/2 cup Fun

3/4 cup Challenge

Sprinkle of Pixie Dust

1. Develop your essential questions for the unit. What do you want students to learn?
2. Create a mission for each one that allows students to demonstrate their learning in a fun and challenging way. Make sure to consider students' access to technology and time that it realistically takes to complete. Consider having different levels students can reach. They don't have to earn experience points for completing this; it could simply be a badge of honor or certificate. These missions are not required. I typically will launch one a week, and I always make sure there is an expiration date and time. How you frame the mission is important; for example, "this week's mission expires at midnight" sounds a lot more exciting than "this week's assignment is due at 4:00 pm."

Other Mission Ideas

- Define the vocabulary terms in the unit in a creative way.
    - Infographic (digital or analog)
    - Movie
    - Slide presentation
    - Snapguide video
    - Google Slides presentation
    - Drawing

The possibilities are endless. Allowing students to demonstrate their learning in a variety of creative ways gives students agency over their learning.

- Create a game to teach this unit's vocabulary terms to class.
- Create a video demonstrating a method learned in this unit and upload it to YouTube.
- Prepare a recipe at home using a method from this unit.
- Create a "sketch-ipe" (visual sketch using a combination of text and images) of a recipe using methods from this unit.

Video Creation

Video creation is an awesome tool for learning in the classroom. There is something about the collaborating and creating when making a video that is magical. One of my favorite uses of video is when students use apps such as iMovie or WeVideo to create promotional videos. At the beginning of the class, I have students create a promotional video introducing their group. This provides a reason for students to get to know one another while doing something fun together. Team members each share something about themselves and wrap it into a fun video, revealing their team name for the semester. Once the videos are created, we play them for the class so everyone gets to know one another. This simple introductory activity also allows students to get comfortable with the technology for future video projects in class.

Another fun project that students enjoy is creating Tasty-style Videos. In 2015, Buzzfeed created a cooking video channel called Tasty that produces captivating viral video tutorials. They currently have over fifty million subscribers on Facebook, and each post receives literally millions of views. The videos feature easy step-by-step recipes in fast motion. The beauty of these videos is that they are quick, delicious looking, and demonstrated in a way that viewers feel empowered to make the recipes.

Many students are familiar with these videos from Facebook, so I thought it would be super fun to create a Tasty-style video in class to demonstrate methods they are learning in class. Allowing students to create step-by-step tutorial videos about their learning allows them to think critically about what they are doing and how to explain it in an easy-to-understand format. Collaboration is essential to this mission, as it takes one person to film, two to stage ingredients and set up the sequence, and one to write the script for each slide. Adding a time requirement adds to the challenge. Give students sixty minutes, and you will you see them amp up their collaboration to another level.

Tasty-style videos are great for cooking but can be used to explain any process. And they don't have to be complex or require a lot of props. *Mental Floss,* a magazine that features random and interesting facts, has created their own style of Tasty tutorial videos using messages written on sticky notes. Check out the video "How Does Disney World Stay So Clean?" to see a thirty-two second example.

The Secret to Keeping Disney Clean

Here's how you can get your students going on a video creation:

Step 1: Decide what you will teach.

What do you want students to demonstrate? Is there something that they could teach? Is there a message they could share? Who will their audience be?

Step 2: Choose a background.

What will the background for your video look like? What would best match the theme of your video? It could be as simple as a student desk, countertop, or floor. What about leaving your class and taking the video production outside, letting nature be the backdrop? Whatever it is, make sure it's clean and consistent throughout.

Step 3: Choose what you'll use to record.

Some of the best videos out there were made with an iPhone, so you definitely don't need to invest in high-quality video equipment. Do you have Chromebooks or iPads? Both would work beautifully to capture video. Tripods take the quality up a notch to ensure a steady capture of video but are not necessary.

Step 4: Speeding things up.

Using fast motion or time-lapse will speed things up to create a short video that takes less time to watch. There are two easy ways to do this: The easiest way is to use the time-lapse feature on your phone or iPad camera app. Look for the "photo" above the found button that takes the picture and swipe until you find "time-lapse." The time-lapse records at 15X speed, so if you film a fifteen-minute video, it will speed it up to one-minute in length. You can also create a fast-motion video by recording your video at normal speed and then speeding it up in iMovie. If you want to slow down a time-lapse video within iMovie, select the segment of the video where you want the speed altered and choose clip from the iMovie menu to access the speed controls.

Step 5: Add background music and edit the video.

Many free online video editors let you add finishing touches to your video, such as YouTube Video Editor, WeVideo, PowToon, or ClipChamp. If you are using an iPhone or iPad, iMovie is intuitive and easy to use. Layering music over content allows students to add that extra bit of personalization to make the video their own. Many video editors have free music you can choose from to add to your video. Check out the wealth of other free music resources available under Creative Commons license to add to your video.

Step 6: Share!

The beauty of today's connected world of social media is that you can share your creations with people from around the world! It is so empowering for students to realize that their videos are not only being shared within the classroom but literally across the globe! Through their videos, they can teach others who may otherwise never have a chance to learn what they have to share.

When students are ready to share their video with the world, they can upload it to social media! Facebook is the platform where Tasty videos are shared, but students can easily share via Twitter, Instagram, or YouTube. Creating a class or team YouTube Channel featuring a collection of these videos is another powerful opportunity to share creations globally with others from around the world.

Stop-Motion Animation

Another wonderful way to make learning magical in your classroom is through stop-motion animation. My students have had a wonderful time creating projects that demonstrate their understanding of the learning targets or standards being taught. In my Culinary 3 class, my students made their own batch of playdough to create a stop-motion video of the cuisine in a part of the world we were studying. Using the DoInk green screen app to create a backdrop, they sculpted their playdough into characters, food, etc., to explain what they had learned. They then used these created animations in their presentations at the end of each unit. There are many apps such as Stikbot Studio or MyStopAction that allow for easy stop-motion creations at most any grade level.

For the Love of Doodling

I've always struggled listening to verbal instructions. I get antsy, my mind wanders, I have a difficult time focusing and retaining the information being shared. Throughout my life, I found myself doodling in class, church, professional development sessions, and anywhere else where I have to sit and listen to someone speak. I draw squiggles, flowers, and other various images on my page with the notes I am taking to help me concentrate on what was being said and find meaning to what I was learning. I also would color my text and images to bring them to life. It wasn't until a few years ago that I realized that there is actually a name for my doodling; it's called sketchnoting. I've since had the opportunity to learn from some amazing authors and educators who have opened my eyes to the power of sketchnoting as a way of capturing text and visuals digitally and on paper to connect and retain information. From my own experience, I knew the incredible potential that sketchnoting could have on learning, and it wasn't long before I decided to get my students sketchnoting too.

Digital or Paper?

When I first began sketchnoting, I tried an app available on iPhone, iPad, or iPod Touch called Paper by 53. This is a wonderful tool to use for visual note-taking. With a variety of pen choices and colors, the app allows for creativity and flexibility. It is user friendly, and I love how it allows you to fix mistakes and publish your creation to Google Classroom or other platforms with ease.

Although I loved the features and user friendliness that Paper53 had to offer, I found that old-fashioned paper worked best for me when I first began. I purchased a square spiral sketchpad, a fine-tip Sharpie, a ton of colored pencils, and I was ready to roll! These compact tools can travel anywhere, and I never have to worry about my battery dying. There is something about coloring that I have always loved, and I really like being able to personalize my font as well as write and draw in fine detail. As I became more comfortable with sketchnoting and found my flow, I returned to Paper53 and absolutely *love* it!

Experiment with a variety of apps and tools and find the best fit. The important thing is that it works for you!

What Should I Sketch?

A few years back, I sat in on a few sketchnoting sessions at various conferences I attended. After these sessions, I decided to get started on my sketchnoting journey. The flexibility and freedom of summer seemed to be the perfect time to put these newly learned skills to practice. I had a stack of new books I wanted to read, and I thought that would be the perfect place to start. As I sketchnoted chapters, I connected my learning at a deeper level and ended up retaining more of the information than I typically did by reading alone; additionally, my sketchnoting practice allowed for creative freedom in my note-taking. I was able to organize and personalize my thoughts in a visually appealing way that I enjoyed looking back at later. I quickly fell in love with this new way of capturing my learning, thoughts, and ideas. Since then, I've sketchnoted PD sessions, TED Talks, and thoughts and ideas that pop into my brain.

Things to Keep in Mind

You don't have to be artistic to sketchnote! If you can draw shapes, lines, and stick figures, you're on your way!

Remember, visual note-taking is a way for you to connect and retain information. No one else has to understand your drawing but you!

Don't worry if sketchnoting doesn't come easily at first! Start with something fun and easy to capture on paper and expand from there! It does get easier, and you will soon find your rhythm and the structure that works best for you. You will also find that each sketchnote takes on a personality of its own, one of my favorite aspects of visually capturing your thoughts and ideas on paper.

The Beauty Is in the Reflection

One of my favorite ways to document my learning during a conference is to sketchnote the sessions and keynotes with visual images and text. I am able to focus better, make deeper connections to the ideas, and retain the information longer when I allow my thoughts to fill the page with images and text. At a recent conference, as one of the last sessions came to a close, I looked at my sketch and realized that although my page was filled with images and text, there was very little color or detail. That's because it wasn't complete. My favorite part of sketchnoting comes after the session; the beauty comes in the reflection.

At times I am able to reflect immediately after the learning, and other times it happens later on the flight home or while I decompress from the experience in my pajamas in the living room. It doesn't matter when it occurs, but it always does. After that particular conference, I settled in at the airport while waiting for my flight, pulled out my iPad Pro, and opened up Paper53 to look at my sketchnotes from the week. With each quote I read and each image I saw, the memories from each session came flooding back, and I began to process what I'd learned. I rewrote some of my text, added in images, wrapped some of my thoughts in containers and bubbles, and I colored.

As a person who recharges in solitude, the act of coloring and creating is therapeutic for me. It brings me back to being a kid sprawled out on my bedroom floor with my big box of crayons and a coloring book. Coloring between the lines and adding my own unique details to the page allowed me to process the day. It gave me time to untangle all of my complicated thoughts and ideas and organize them into manageable chunks. This is exactly what happens when I reflect on my sketchnotes. I am able to take the new ideas and content, connect them to prior knowledge, and sort them out into manageable chunks of information that are meaningful and actionable. I also find that taking the time to make my sketches visually appealing brings me joy. Like a photograph, it captures a memorable moment in time that I want to revisit.

When I teach sketchnoting to my students, I share the importance of the reflection time. I tell them to not worry so much about adding color and detail when they are documenting their learning. If it helps them focus, they can do it. If it distracts them from making connections and paying attention to what they are learning, they can wait until after class. I always try to carve out a minimum of ten minutes for students to process what they have sketched, add details, color, and ask questions of those around them to fill in missing information or make sense of what they recorded in their notes. I have found that my students really appreciate this time. Just as I do, they find this time of reflection to be valuable for connecting and sorting their new ideas and organizing them into chunks that are meaningful and actionable. Some students prefer to complete their sketches at home in solitude, which is just fine by me.

Some people feel that if they can't draw images and text, color, and make it beautiful before the learning is over, sketchnoting isn't for them. I thought this too, at first; however, I know now that this just isn't how I process. I need time to reflect, sort, organize, and color. My sketchnotes have evolved over time as I've developed my own style and flow. The more I sketch, the more I love it and appreciate how valuable it is to my learning. I also find it's a way for me to give back to those who have shared their heart and passion as well as share to those who were unable to take part in the experience.

Unleashing the Power of Sketchnoting on My Students

Visual note-taking has truly allowed me to connect my thoughts and ideas in meaningful ways, more effectively helping me to retain information and make more sense of my learning. It has been so powerful for me in my personal learning, so I was determined to find a way to teach this method of note-taking to my students. I had created opportunities for my students to sketchnote multiple times but never really felt that I front-loaded it effectively . . . until recently.

I was inspired by visual thinker and author of *The Doodle Revolution,* Sunni Brown, at a session I attended at IntegratED in Portland, Oregon, and was ready to try a new approach to teaching this visual note-taking strategy to students. To be completely honest, this was one of those lightbulb moments where I made a last-minute change to my lesson in the final hour before class. It was a risk but one that ended up being a huge success.

My students had just finished making a rich dough that they were going to be storing to make doughnuts the next day. As they were coming back to their tables after cleanup, I had cups of freshly sharpened colored pencils, black pens, one index card, and one square piece of drawing paper waiting for each student. To begin, I showed them my collection of sketchnotes and shared my personal journey in visual note-taking and how it has been a powerful way for me to connect my learning and retain information. I explained how learning this method of visual note-taking would provide them with another tool that they could use not only in this class but also in other classes and experiences as well.

To introduce the basics of visual note-taking, I used Matt Miller's slideshow "Sketchnotes: Tools and Tactics for Visual Note-taking" from the *Ditch that Textbook* website. I found this slideshow very helpful, and it included a video clip called "Sketcho Frenzy" that explains sketchnoting basics beautifully.

Now it was time for an activity. In her session, Sunni had attendees participate in an activity where she called out an item, and we had to draw it and then pass our paper around the table until we got it back so we could see everyone else's drawing. We repeated this with six or seven more items, each getting slightly more abstract as we went. I really liked how this activity made you think about how you would draw different images and allowed you to see how different people perceive images in different ways. I walked my students through this activity on their index cards, and they *loved* it! They were completely engaged and had so much fun! It also relaxed them and gave them a bit of confidence to begin our first sketchnote.

Students were now warmed up and ready for me to walk them through the sketchnote process. I shared with them how I use a black pen to write text and images and colored pencils to shade and add color. I created a slideshow with each instruction on a different slide. The first step was to write "Yeast Bread Method" on their piece of drawing paper. It could be placed anywhere they wanted based on the structure that they wanted to set up on their page. Next I showed them "Step 1" of the yeast bread method. I asked them what images came to mind. I had them add text and images on their page for "Step 1," thinking about their placement based on their sketchnote structure. I then proceeded to "Step 2," "Step 3," etc. until all steps were included. I told students that if they were done before we moved on to the next step, they could use the time to add color, detail, etc. You could hear a pin drop in the room. Students were completely immersed in their drawings.

To finish, we discussed how they felt about this new method of note-taking, and students had wonderful ideas about how they could use this in other areas of their lives. It was interesting to hear students say how much they enjoyed it, but they voiced concern that it wouldn't be an accepted form of note-taking by some teachers, or they feared that they wouldn't get enough information down. We had a great discussion about whether it was more valuable to record lots of information or truly comprehend, connect, and retain what was learned.

After this lesson, I was inspired to continue practicing visual note-taking with my students. It is such an important skill that we can equip our students with and use in all subject areas and experiences. I encourage you to take the leap and think about how you may be able to incorporate sketchnoting into your own personal learning and/or your classroom. To learn more about sketchnoting, follow Carrie Baughcum (@heckawesome) and Monica Spillman (@mospillman). They are wonderfully supportive and are always sharing amazing blogs, vlogs, and challenges.

It is so important for us as educators to model what it looks like to try new things and venture into the unknown. I have never had a student criticize me for trying something new, and often times it is quite the contrary. I have found students really appreciate a teacher who is continuously wanting to improve and move beyond the status quo in the classroom. After all, that's where the magic happens.

Collaborative Engagement

Collaboration has always been a part of my culinary classes. I have eight kitchens, so students work in teams on a daily basis. I have formulated my student teams in a myriad of ways throughout my past fifteen years of teaching because each class is unique and brings its own special flavor. In some classes, I've selected teams; in others, I've let them select their own and every other variation in between.

The most important thing I've found to create a powerful team dynamic is building relationships from day one. As I mentioned in Memorable Beginnings, the first two weeks are all about creating a classroom culture. In those early days of the semester, students change groups every day to get used to working with a variety of people. Allowing time for your students to gel as a class will pay off dividends in the long run. You will find they will go deeper with their learning when they feel it's safe to take risks and explore with students they trust.

As part of our Memorable Beginnings, students spend a few weeks relationship building before we start settling into teams. The Draft has worked beautifully in my classes, but prior to that, I chose teams a bit differently. I would put a paper up in each of the kitchens, and students could pick where they wanted to go. I gave them a heads-up a few days prior so they could be thinking about it. Believe me, I've gone round and round on whether this was a good idea to let students choose groups or just choose for them. I've done it every way imaginable. What I've found is giving students adequate time to get to know various students in the room allows them to connect and find out the best dynamic for them. Of course, I have students who don't care where they go. I tell those students to let me know, and I will place them where there is room. Are there ever issues with personality conflicts? Absolutely. But allowing students the autonomy to select their groups eliminates about ninety-five percent of those conflicts. Conflict resolution is an important part of the learning, so when they arise, I help to give them the tools to work it out among their team.

Teams in my classes are never more than four. I have found three to four students to be ideal. Each student has a role, and all have a part to play in the creating. Less creates unnecessary stress because there is more to do than what time will allow for. More than that and there isn't enough for everyone to take part in.

So much critical communication and thinking go on during the creating process when students are collaborating in teams. Students get totally immersed in the activities of decoding recipes together, discussing, sharing, and troubleshooting. It's truly magical to see this powerful team dynamic in action.

Creating an Identity

Allowing students to own their experience in my class is an important piece in student engagement. When teams are created, they create a team name and promo video. Not only does this allow students to bond as a team, it creates an identity within my class. My kitchens are color coded, so to save my sanity, I have students incorporate the kitchen color into their team name, e.g., Rockin' Red Tomatoes, Purple Pistachios, etc. Including the color name eliminates confusion for other teams and me, especially in the beginning as our class is getting to know one another. Allowing for this creativity goes a long way in student buy in. Since they all collaborated on developing a team name and promotional video, they immediately feel a bond and connection to other team members. There is pride in establishing an identity that continues to build over the course of the semester.

Another important piece in building collaboration within the team is helping students find their purpose. When students realize that their unique personalities, passions, and strengths bring value to the team, it changes the way they engage and collaborate with their teammates. Students become more encouraging and positive, and they bring out the best in one another. They realize that their team and classmates are counting on them, and the experience is not the same without them there. They find their purpose, voice, and value. This is employability skill-building in action. Isn't this what we want students to be able to do in life—work collaboratively and bring out one another's best? When we create opportunities for students to do this in our classes, we are helping to build skills that are going to be essential throughout life.

Every team is going to hit roadblocks and frustrations in learning. Being part of a team that backs one another through the struggles is huge. Each member is an important piece to the puzzle, and it's crucial that all support and encourage one another every step of the way. This increases trust and deepens their bond. As they overcome obstacles, they become more unified as a team.

We are all better together. I know that having people in my educational journey who know my passions and strengths helps encourage and push me to take greater leaps of faith. In the same ways, helping our students build relationships with their peers will give them confidence to keep learning and leaping.

The Introvert

Creating a classroom where collaboration is key may at first seem like a deterrent for the introverted student. My experience has proven the opposite to be true. I have found the secret to helping introverts flourish in a collaborative class is to be intentional about creating a completely safe place where their voice is valued. I myself am an introvert. As a student, I was cautious about sharing my thoughts and opinions in fear they would be rejected or laughed at. Often I would keep my thoughts to myself only to be internally kicking myself when others were applauded for sharing thoughts and ideas similar to my own. It's taken a long time to develop the courage and confidence to share, and still, more often than I'd like to admit, I revert back to that younger Tisha who second-guessed her value. Knowing this about myself, I am very intentional about creating an atmosphere and culture where students not only feel safe but also valued to share their voice.

Using digital tools like Flipgrid, Padlet, and other collaborative tools helps introverts find and share their voice. It is a little less intimidating to some to share written words rather than verbal ones at times. When peers and teachers validate their thoughts and ideas with meaningful feedback, those students who feared sharing gain the confidence to risk sharing again.

When introverted students realize they are valued and a critical component to the class dynamic, they feel safe and empowered. They begin believing in themselves and what they are capable of doing. That's when students go from passive participants to active leaders. Time and time again I have found that it is the introverted student who finds his or her place and passion in my culinary classes. I will always treasure a letter I received from a precious student who had spent four years in my culinary classes. She began her freshman year as a timid, insecure freshman and blossomed into a courageous leader as she graduated her senior year on her way to start culinary school. The words of her letter touched my heart in a profound way, but these words melted me: "In your class I found my passion and realize I can chase my wildest dreams." What better gift could I be given as a teacher than a student sharing with me that, in my class, she was given the opportunity to chase her wildest dreams?

Listening in a World of Distractions

More and more I've come to understand that listening is one of the most important things we can do for one another. Whether the other be an adult or a child, our engagement in listening to who that person is can often be our greatest gift. Whether that person is speaking or playing or dancing, building or singing or painting, if we care, we can listen.

–Fred Rogers

We live in a world of distractions. Our senses are being bombarded continually from every angle. As I am writing right now, I find myself glancing at my phone notifications, thinking about my unfinished to-do list, listening to the hum of the washing machine, and wondering how long it will be until I'm going to need to start a new load. Most of the time, we aren't even aware of all that pulls at our focus and attention from one moment to the next until we stop and intentionally pay attention to them.

My mind goes a million miles per minute. I am a highly sensitive, intuitive being who takes in every emotion of the world around me. The blessing is that I'm able to sense problems and emotions before others and react to them quickly. The curse is that my senses operate on overload most of the time, and I not only become distracted but overwhelmed by all that is coming at me. If I'm not careful, I find myself hearing but not truly listening, because my mind is busy processing past conversations, smells, noises, you name it! I am working on learning to be present at all times. Let me tell you, it is not easy! But the more intentional I am about listening for understanding and pushing back the distractions, the more I enjoy the world around me.

Listening and being present has become a critical component to my joy-filled classroom. In my culinary class, any number of distractions can keep me from my main focus: students. With laundry, dishes, ingredients to prep, etc., there are many things vying for my attention. To help minimize those distractions for myself, I have a Sous Chef—a student helper—in every class. They sign up for the position as a class credit, and they are responsible for helping manage the kitchen as well as mentor students. Creating this position for students has freed me up to facilitate learning and building relationships with students, and it gives students an opportunity to refine their culinary and employability skills and become leaders. My Sous Chefs assist me with giving feedback when students present their finished product at the end of the period. Giving students the opportunity to critically think about the food they are evaluating and articulate their feedback to other students reinforces their learning and develops their communication skills. I find that students give amazing feedback, sometimes even more detailed and specific than mine. Students listen carefully to what their peers say and are receptive to the feedback given.

While my Sous Chef oversees classroom upkeep, I rotate around the room and interact with students. This allows me to identify specific learning needs, check for understanding, formatively assess students' skills, and help them tap into their curiosity and creativity. More importantly, I am able to encourage and support them as well as get to know them not only as learners but as people. Students are much more likely to listen and learn from you if they know you are truly listening and care about them. By asking them about their days, their interests, or their other classes, they see that I care about them beyond what is happening in the classroom. When we take the time to listen, we are able to understand so much about the students we serve. We are much more likely to sense when students are "off" or having a bad day. So many meltdowns and explosions have been prevented simply because I know my students well enough to stop, listen, and react accordingly to help de-escalate the situation.

We will always be bombarded by distractions. As educators, we have to remember that our students should always be our focus. When we are intentional about being present and giving our students our full attention, it pays off dividends in the long run. I'm not going to pretend it's easy. It's a continual struggle, and there are days I blow it and let the distractions get the best of me. Finding ways to minimize the madness that threatens our focus so we can listen with intention and be present can be our greatest gift to the students we serve.

Runza

When I think about my journey as a connected educator, I am in awe. It's difficult to put into words how powerful it is to connect with a community that feeds and shares your passion. I'm daily inspired, challenged, and encouraged by people who have not only become my professional learning network (PLN), but also my friends. Over the years, I've become more and more comfortable sharing my educational experiences through Twitter as a way to give back to educators who are continually sharing with me. I can't overstate the value it has brought to my teaching. It tears down school walls and allows others in to observe other ways of doing things, to expand perspectives, generate ideas, and challenge the status quo. By being vulnerable and sharing a piece of our educational story, we can't help but grow. It forces us to reflect on our own teaching practice in a new way and makes us realize what is ordinary and routine for us could indeed be ground-breaking and pivotal in someone else's journey. It may, in fact, be the catalyst that sparks a reaction to shift one's practice and mindset. One of my favorite YouTube clips is "Obvious to you. Amazing to Others" by Derek Sivers. In this clip, Sivers says, "Everybody's ideas seem obvious to them; I'll bet even John Coltrain or Richard Feinman felt that everything they were playing or saying was pretty obvious, so maybe what's obvious to me is amazing to someone else." As teachers, we continually refine our practice and discover strategies, methods, tips, and tricks that our students respond to, and they become second nature to us in how we teach. They become so integral in our daily teaching that we don't even think about it. It's obvious to us. We need to share because our obvious may be someone else's lightbulb moment.

Time and time again, I've been in awe of the response I get from my PLN when I have a question or need suggestions. One of my favorite examples of this was a result of me asking about a Runza. For those of you who don't know, a Runza is a Nebraskan delicacy made of a warm bun stuffed with peppery beef, wilted cabbage, and sautéed onions. In Culinary 3, we spend a semester learning about American regional cuisine. We were in the Midwestern part of the United States, and I was looking for recipes for Midwestern favorites that my students had not heard of or experienced. I remembered my friend, Craig Badura, mentioning a Runza in a Twitter conversation and decided to reach out and see if he could suggest a recipe that we could use in class so that my students in Southern Oregon could experience a taste of the Midwest. This is where the magic happened. Craig jokingly tweeted back, "I wonder if @runza could help a class in Southern Oregon out." It was within the day that I received a reply back from Runza: "Send us a DM, and we'll send you Runzas!" What?! A simple tweet resulted in a company sending our class a box of Runzas straight from their store! Within a week, a box of Runzas, frozen solid from being shipped on dry ice, arrived in our school office. Our kids not only had the experience of making their own Runzas, but they were also able to experience an actual piece of Nebraskan tradition first-hand!

Don't underestimate the power of connections. We live in a time where we can literally connect with people from around the world in extraordinary ways. Don't miss the opportunity to expand your horizons, challenge your practice, and share a piece of your journey with the world. You never know how your "ordinary" could be someone else's "amazing."

Curiosity

We keep moving forward, opening new doors, and doing things because we're curious, and curiosity keeps leading us down new paths.

–Walt Disney

When we tap into curiosity, we experience the sheer joy of discovery. When I transition from baking and pastry to culinary arts at the end of the first quarter, I tell students that, above all else, by the end of the quarter, I want them to open up their refrigerators and cupboards at home and get excited about the possibilities to create something amazing with the ingredients they see there. I want them to feel confident in their skills and free to infuse their own personalities and styles to their cooking. I view the skills that they learn in my class as a foundation that they will build on for a lifetime. The memories they make in my class are going to stay with them. If those memories are good, my students will most likely have positive associations with cooking. If the memories are bad, those associations are going to be negative, and they likely won't have interest in building on those skills in the future. Creating an atmosphere of curiosity where students feel safe to explore and play is vital to building confidence and ownership of learning.

Here's an example of how I create this type of atmosphere of curiosity and exploration in my class: In Culinary Arts 2, I teach students how to make one of the five Mother Sauces: Béchamel. They prepare the sauce and turn it into a Mornay (Cheese) sauce to make macaroni and cheese. They learn the fundamentals, and I give them authentic, immediate feedback on the dish's taste, texture, and appearance. Once they learn the skill, it is time to take it to the next level and make it their own. The next day, I provide a variety of herbs, spices, vegetables, and cheeses for them to experiment with. They can create anything they want from the ingredients available. As students are sent to their kitchens, their creative juices start flowing. Their curiosity is piqued as they smell and taste the ingredients, discussing, googling, and experimenting with flavor combinations. An electricity fills the room as the Four Cs work in perfect unison. Everywhere you turn, students are immersed in collaboration, creation, critical thinking, and communication. More importantly, they are smiling, laughing, and having fun! Now don't get me wrong . . . they are seriously learning, but they are playing as well. Walt Disney says it best: "It's kind of fun to do the impossible."

When students bring me their creations for evaluation at the end of the class period, the expressions on their faces are priceless. They are so proud to show me their dishes. I love to hear their descriptions and explanations of what they have created. You can hear a pin drop as I take my first bite; students can't wait to hear what I have to say. The feedback I give is immediate and honest. I explain in detail the flavors, the textures, and the appearance of the dish I am experiencing. I ask questions. I express what I love and give tips on how it could be improved. This reflection time validates the students and gives them the chance to discuss the struggles, victories, failures, and successes. They are able to think through what went right, what went wrong, and how they could improve next time. The learning is rich, relevant, and meaningful. By taking a skill they learned and making it their own, they now will have confidence to go home and open their own cupboards and refrigerators and create something amazing. I especially love to hear my students say they are going to make the dish for their family for dinner.

The magical classroom is one where students are safe, valued, immersed, and empowered. There is curiosity and wonder. They are creating, collaborating, critically thinking, and communicating. It is the maker of memories, laughter, and fun.

Mystery and Wonder

Creating classrooms that are full of the joy and the wonder of learning is a passion of mine. I am continually pondering new ways to make my classroom a magical space. I think many teachers have the same desire. We want to create powerful experiences for our students, but it is easy to overthink it. We become so overwhelmed by the idea of doing something so incredible and mind blowing with our students that we become paralyzed and end up not doing anything different at all. What I've discovered is that sometimes all it takes is a little mystery and wonder to take a lesson from ordinary to amazing.

I've added a bit of mystery and wonder in a number of ways, but today all it took was a Google Form. In Culinary Arts 3, we are beginning a new unit on Midwestern cuisine. Our food truck teams have been traveling across the country from Medford, Oregon, to Medford, Maine, and we've arrived in the Midwest. To create a little excitement when they returned on the first day back from winter break, I had a YouTube clip with adventure music playing in the background and this message on the screen in front of the room. "Your food trucks have arrived in the Midwest! To discover your first recipe . . . you must unlock the clues!!! Jump into Google Classroom . . . your adventure begins now." When students entered class, a buzz of excitement was immediately generated. Students quickly gathered iPads and teamed up to begin unlocking the clues.

All I used to generate the clues was a Google Form. I came up with five clues that they would unlock to reveal the Midwestern recipe they were preparing for the day. I've included a YouTube video explaining how I created this below.

It was so fun to see students collaborating to unlock each clue. One iPad on each team had a Google Form opened while the others were used for Google searches. It took teams between fifteen to twenty minutes to unlock all of the clues that led to their recipe. To personalize your specific set of circumstances, you could add more or less clues and increase or decrease the complexity to fit the time frame you have to work with. My Google Form led students to a recipe upon submission, but yours could lead to a YouTube clip or other activity depending on what you teach.

Adding this little bit of mystery and wonder took my lesson from ordinary to amazing without a whole lot of effort. Not only did students start class more energized, they also began collaborating and thinking more quickly than they would have otherwise. The built-in anticipation that it generated created a buzz and excitement, and students could hardly wait to begin preparing their recipes! Have you guessed what it is they made?? Remember the story I shared earlier about the special Nebraskan delivery? You guessed it, they made a Runza!

Mystery Badges

Another way I've incorporated mystery and wonder into my classroom is by creating Mystery Badges. Up to this point, the badges I've awarded in my class have all had experience points attached with varying amounts that are visible to them when they are earned. This mechanic has worked really well in my class as students collect badges to reach Line Cook, Sous Chef, and ultimately, MasterChef status; however, as I watched my students interact with the game, I realized for the first time with that unit that what we were missing was a little mystery.

The magic of a gamified classroom is in adding twists and turns and a little mystery whenever you want. So when this unit started, I threw them a curveball. I told them that I would be awarding Mystery Badges throughout the unit that would each hold an XP amount behind a scratch off sticker. Students would not be able to reveal the scratch off amount until the end of the unit when all the badges were turned in. This little bit of anticipation adds a new excitement to the game! They can only strategize so much because there is an element of chance that won't be revealed until the end. I knew, by my students' responses when I revealed this new mechanic, that this was going to bring a whole new dimension to our classroom dynamic. They were excited!

Just like my other badges, I create them in Pages on iOS. I make each badge the size of a baseball card so students can keep them in a plastic baseball card sleeve. I then laminate the page and cut out the badges. Once the badges are laminated and cut, I apply a scratch off sticker to each one. Adding the sticker to a laminated surface allows the badges to be reused by removing the remainder of scratch off and applying a new sticker; however, you could apply the sticker directly to a badge printed on cardstock and left unlaminated, but it would just prevent them from being reused. Either way works!

The Mystery Badges are kept in a box, and when students earn one, they reach in and pick one randomly. The badges hold various amounts of experience points behind the sticker: 250, 500, 1,000, and 1,500. To make the higher XP a little harder to get, I populate the box with more of the lower numbers incrementally and the fewest badges holding 1,500. This balances out the XP and makes it a big deal when the higher amount is revealed. Again, they can't scratch off the amount till the end of the unit, so it adds another layer of suspense!

The beauty of gamification is you don't have to have everything figured out from the get-go! You can add mechanics to your game as you observe how your students interact with it. If things get a little predictable, add a new element to mix things up. If certain player types aren't buying in, find a mechanic to bring them on board. YOU are the game designer! Adding twists and turns and a bit of Mystery keeps the game exciting! Who doesn't love a good mystery?!

Connect and Collaborate

We've talked a bit about collaboration inside the classroom, but as a connected educator, I know there is huge value to collaborating with those outside our classroom. Some of that happens when community members visit our classrooms as special guests or judges. Collaboration can also happen on a national and even global scale. There was a time when I taught in isolation. I was a singleton educator teaching a subject that I didn't think anyone else could relate to. I mean, really? Could anyone relate to a teacher that handed out Chef's knives to her students? So I went on minding my own business, isolated in my culinary Narnia.

Enter the Twittersphere. Since I began connecting on Twitter four years ago, I have come to realize that I can learn so much from teachers of all subjects and grade levels. I am continually inspired and challenged in my teaching practice, taking ideas from a myriad of subject areas and finding new ways to infuse them into my classroom. I have learned that expanding my perspective beyond my narrow culinary vision allows me to think differently about content and what is possible. My PLN has become a family that I have turned to time and time again for not only ideas but also inspiration, wisdom, support, and encouragement. It's safe to say that I have grown more as an educator the past four years than I have my seventeen years of teaching combined. Sound crazy? Yes. Crazy awesome, that is!

So what happens when, in this crazy, awesome world, you find other teachers from across the United States that ARE just like you: teachers who hand out Chef's knives to their students too? Let me tell you—it rocks your world! It's so incredible, in fact, that I started a Voxer group where we all could connect and idea share to our heart's content! Culinary Powers, Activate! If you aren't following Julie Rice, Kelleigh Ratzlaff, or Karyn McAllister . . . stop everything and follow them now! They are amazing culinary educators who are continually blowing my mind with their amazing ideas and passion for education!

This past summer, we decided to all collaborate on an idea we had wanted to try but hadn't . . . a culinary escape room! I had always dreamed of taking this project on, but for some reason, the thought of creating a game from scratch paralyzed me; however, taking on this endeavor as a team felt much less daunting. We all set up a time to meet via Google Hangout to idea share and delegate tasks. We created a Google doc to collaborate and brainstorm and then followed one another's progress on Voxer. I will tell you that this collaboration process was FANTASTIC! Kelleigh created a Google Site to house the digital escape room, and Julie, Karyn, and she created content, clues, and codes. It was truly awe-inspiring to watch it all come together.

We launched the digital escape room at different times, and it was so helpful to share our reflections of how the game played out. As everyone shared, we were able to anticipate possible glitches or issues and prepare for them ahead of time. It was also wonderful to share frustrations and successes with one another as the adventures unfolded. We were able to provide encouragement, support, and suggestions because we all had taken part in the process.

This collaboration was much more than creating an escape room. It was forming a bond with other educators that were on a similar adventure as my own. Was this escape room the only thing we discussed throughout the past month? No. We shared other lessons, strategies, documents, and links. We talked about family and celebrated victories and frustrations. We were sharing life together and the treasure that is found in being connected. This experience brought me closer to a group of friends that I'm so grateful to be on this educational journey with. I have a feeling that our adventures are just beginning.

Global Collaboration

This year as I launched into our semester on International Cuisine, I knew it was time to take learning to the next level and try something new. If we were going to be "racing" across the globe learning about food from around the world, what better way to make our learning relevant than to collaborate with others who were experiencing that cuisine.

The only thing holding me back was fear. I had never done anything like this before and wasn't sure how to go about it. I sent out a few tweets reaching out to my PLN in hopes that some other educators would want to join forces with us, and sure enough, I received some replies! Brandi Miller, a first-grade teacher in Florida, and Stephanie Crawford, an eighth-grade teacher in Chicago, Illinois, both said they'd love to collaborate with us in our Amazing Race adventures. I began a Voxer Chat with each of them and began brainstorming what this could look like. As we shared back and forth through our Voxer conversations, our plan started to take shape. Because we were on different zones, it was difficult to communicate via Google Hangout, so we decided to start a Flipgrid to share videos back and forth.

Each first grader sent us an introduction video stating their name, where they were from, their favorite food, and my students sent one back. My high school students had so much fun with this! They loved seeing the personalities of each of the first graders and were anxious to reply. Brandi divided her class into groups of three or four to partner with my students, and each of her teams researched the countries my students were learning about in the game. Each of her student teams created a Google slide that my students could incorporate into their presentations at the Pit Stop at the end of the leg; additionally, when my students prepared international dishes in class for our mini challenges, they created a "foodsnap" and uploaded it to a Padlet. We shared the link with Brandi's classes, and they voted on their favorites using the "star" feature. Teams scoring the most stars earned extra "miles" within the race leg. Brandi said her kids loved being a part of this experience and having a voice in how my students were evaluated, and my kids loved that they were involved too.

Our eighth-grade collaboration started out similarly with a slightly different focus. The eighth graders were studying marketing, so I thought it would be great fun to have them create logo designs for each team. Stefanie divided her students up and matched them with our teams to create logo designs. My students shared their promotional videos with them to introduce their team as well as a short introduction on Flipgrid to share their vision for a logo design. Stefanie's eighth graders watched them and sent a video back asking follow-up questions and sharing their ideas.

It's so fun to see this collaboration blossom between three classes of various ages in three different time zones. There is no limit to the collaborations that are possible in our globally connected world. Tear down your classroom walls and reach out, and you will be amazed at how powerful the learning can be for you and your students!

Make Something Magical

- ✳ What are some ways you could incorporate more making into your class? What could students create to explore your content?
- ✳ Have you ever tried sketchnoting? How might you use this processing method with your students?
- ✳ What are the challenges you've dealt with regarding teams and collaboration in your classroom? What ideas do you have for resolving those issues?
- ✳ How can you involve students in your classroom routines so that you can be freed to focus on your students?
- ✳ How can you increase collaboration with others outside your classroom?
- ✳ How could you add a little bit of wonder to your classroom?

Chapter 7
Authentic Audience

As a Career and Technical Education teacher, my job is to prepare students for a career in the restaurant and hospitality field. Creating experiences that are real and relevant and preparing them for post-secondary education is very important. I also have articulation agreements with a local college, so students who are completing our program get College Now credit. With this alignment of our standards, it is critical that I prepare my students with the skills that are going to keep them in line with students who are taking the classes at the college level. Creating learning experiences that are meaningful and relevant is essential for keeping the integrity of our programs.

One way to create relevancy is by connecting with community partners. Reaching out to local businesses allows us to develop relationships with our community, so students have a pulse on the local industry in our area. Many students are already working in jobs in hospitality, so this is a benefit to them now as well as post-graduation.

I make it a point to introduce myself to local business owners to establish connections and build relationships. Recently, though, I decided to take a different approach to connecting. Instead of making all the connections myself, I decided to have the students make them! I created postcards using Canva with an explanation of our upcoming Food Truck Race. I included my contact information and wrote various local food trucks on each one. The next day in class, I told my students that I wanted them to pick two postcards. They were going on an Adventure Quest. They were to visit local food trucks and deliver the cards to the owners. Upon delivery, students were to introduce themselves and explain the class project. If they took a selfie with the food truck owner, they would get a grocery money incentive towards their next challenge. If the food truck owner actually contacted me and agreed to come into class to either present or judge, they would get an additional bonus.

This was a game changer for my students and me! Students were now the ones making the connections, which was much more meaningful than if I had done it. In the process, they were learning speaking skills, professionalism, and actually meeting business owners face-to-face in their place of employment. The business owners who contacted me were extremely impressed with my students' enthusiasm and professionalism and were eager to help.

Creating opportunities for industry partners and staff members to take part in the learning has made a profound impact in my classroom. Students' skills are amplified when they are creating for an authentic audience of adults whom they admire and respect. Two of my favorite classroom experiences are our MasterChef and Food Truck challenges. I send out email invites to our staff members, district administrators, and local restaurant owners, inviting them to take part as judges. Within this email is a Google form for them to sign up for time slots and sometimes a video trailer, giving them a little taste of the epic experience that awaits them. When I send these invites, the response is immediate! People jump at the opportunity to be judges and watch students shine.

On MasterChef challenge day, students enter the room with their game faces on and are ready to roll. They immediately begin setting up their spaces so they are prepared and ready when the timer starts. The team dynamic kicks into full gear as students collaborate, communicate, and critically think with high-level creative intensity.

With about ten minutes remaining on the clock, judges come in to a table set with everything they need for serious food tasting and evaluating: plates, napkins, pen and rubric for scoring, and a glass of water. I make this as legitimate as possible, so all participants feel the importance of the event. I always offer to prepare coffee for our guest judges as well and make them feel welcome. I am very aware they are taking valuable time out of their day to participate, and I want to make sure they know how much we appreciate it.

Teams present in the order that they finish their dish preparation the day of our MasterChef Challenges. When the buzzer signals that time's up, each team brings their finished creation to the judging table and explains what they made and how they prepared it. I tell students they need to "sell it," and they do! Students approach the table with such pride. They are empowered learners who have made something mind blowing, and they can't wait to share! What I love about this is often our judges include other teachers and staff members whom our students know in a completely different context. Often my students struggle in other classes but shine in my class. To have the opportunity to present their creations and show their skill and creativity to adults they admire is a really big deal. Their expressions as they bring their dishes to the judging table are priceless.

As students explain their creations, judges are tasting and evaluating them based on taste, texture, and appearance. Students hover

over the judging table like their lives depend on the outcome. The feedback from the judges is authentic and so meaningful to my students. They hang on to every word and go back to their kitchens to reflect, discuss, and clean.

Once all the judging has been completed, I tally the scores to determine the ranking of each group. When students come into class the next day, I announce the top three teams and award them badges for their achievement. I also hand back all of the scoring sheets from the judges, giving them time to read and reflect on the judge's feedback. I spend time during the period, rotating from group to group and discussing the feedback and the group's thoughts on the overall experience. This reflection time allows teams to celebrate their successes and think through what they could do to improve their performance and product. It's powerful!

Our Food Truck Challenges are very similar; however, instead of setting up a judging table, judges come in as customers and rotate around the room visiting each food truck station. Food truck owners (a.k.a. students) set up their signature dishes and promotional videos explaining the cuisine of the region we are visiting. Customers are handed clipboards with rubrics to score and write feedback as well as $2,000 of play money to allocate to the team scoring highest on their food truck presentations. The customers are a mix of staff and district employees as well as local restaurant and food truck owners. It is incredibly powerful to have adults whom students admire taste their dishes and hear them present on the regional cuisine and flavor profiles of the region. The customers ask clarifying questions, and students are prepared with their answers. Students know the importance of their research because they are going to be quizzed by people they respect and admire. They want to be prepared because they want to impress!

I love the feedback and ideas that customers give during these challenges as well. Local restaurant owners give real and relevant feedback on how teams can streamline production, cut costs, or improve the flavor, texture, and appearance of their food. Let me tell you, when a chef gives feedback to students on ways to improve their food quality and efficiency, they listen! The advice that comes from respected adults at their school is equally valuable. They care what they have to say and love that staff members they love took the time to take part in the experience.

The growth I see in my students from the beginning of the semester to the end is extraordinary! When students present for their first challenge, they are timid and quiet. They are difficult to understand and lack confidence. Each of the six challenges brings increased confidence, and by the end of the semester, they are more poised, prepared, articulate, and their pride and skill shine through. It truly is an amazing transformation to witness.

The community was thrilled to be a part of this learning experience for my students. To be completely honest, I was nervous the first time we invited people from outside our school. *What would these local chefs think of my students' skills? Would they think I've been preparing them all wrong? Would they think this Amazing Food Truck Race idea was crazy?* But this was, in my mind, the best way to allow for authentic learning. Inviting chefs, who are out there every day in the restaurant industry, to come in and give feedback to my students could take their learning to a much higher level.

This is twenty-first-century learning in action.

This is what it looks like to have learning come alive.

When Our Students Are the Audience

My Culinary 3 and 4 students are combined into the same class period but work independently from one another within my class. While my Culinary 3 students are learning regional and international cuisine, my Culinary 4 students work at their own pace on passion projects. I love to include my Culinary 4 students as judges on mini-challenge days in Culinary 3, and they love it too. Just as with the MasterChef and Food Truck Challenges, the judges take a seat at the judging table where they evaluate each team's dish as it is presented.

The first time I involved my students as judges, I knew it was a good decision. The students (from both classes) took it seriously. My Culinary 4 student judges discussed each dish in detail and gave very specific and descriptive feedback. Even as they were helping my Culinary 3 students improve their work, they, too, were practicing important skills. Giving them this responsibility to evaluate and share their feedback was a valuable experience for them.

The Ultimate Summative Assessment

Not long ago, I had the honor of taking four fabulous culinary students up to Lane Community College in Eugene, Oregon, for a culinary competition. Each group of two had submitted a menu for Round 1 of the competition and had been selected among many other high school culinary students to move on to Round 2.

As we made the early morning drive to Eugene, I wondered, *Did I prepare them enough? Did they prepare enough? How is their level of skill going to match up to the other competitors?*

When we arrived, my students received a brand new knife kit and chef's coat for winning Round 1 of the competition. My students unwrapped each knife, reveling in the fact that they had *earned* them because of what they had accomplished.

The moments leading up to the competition start time were filled with anticipation. My students worried about whether they would be able to identify all of the products, complete the math problems, and be able to create a meal from the black box of ingredients provided. Our conversation was filled with words of reassurance and last-minute discussions over Google searches.

The students were led back to the culinary classrooms by the instructors, and spectators were left in a room with a screen projecting a live stream of the competition. As the challenge was revealed, my students quickly discussed what needed to be done and got to work. I was impressed with how they worked under pressure as the judges watched their every move and asked them questions while they prepared the food. To be honest, it was hard to watch. I so wanted to hear what they were saying and be able to give them encouragement and little words of wisdom. But this was their time, and it was the ultimate summative assessment during which they had to demonstrate how well they could apply their skills—in an intense challenge in front of an audience of chef instructors.

When my students came back from the challenge, they looked exhausted, but their sense of accomplishment was palpable. One even said, "I don't care how well we did; I'm so proud of us!" Those words melted my heart; I was proud of them too.

The afternoon seemed to drag on forever as we awaited the competition results. When the moment finally came and two of the four were announced as first place winners, we could all hardly believe it. I was so incredibly proud and excited for my students but, at the same time, feeling sad for the two that didn't place. I wasn't quite sure how they were going to react.

This is when I realized the power of this authentic experience. The two that didn't take first place embraced the winners with genuine love and excitement. They were all a team. It didn't matter if one team came home with a higher ranking than another. They had accomplished something incredible. They had succeeded in demonstrating their understanding under extremely difficult circumstances and had overcome serious obstacles. Although the extrinsic award was great, the intrinsic reward proved much greater.

On the drive home, one of my students told me, "When I signed up for Culinary my freshman year, I didn't know if I would like it. I was an introvert and didn't know if I would enjoy working in a group. But I have made incredible friendships and have learned and grown so much by working together as a team. Culinary is my place now; it is home." Those words will stay with me for a very long time. This is a perfect example of how powerful it is when we create authentic experiences for students.

Collaboration. Problem Solving. Relevance. Growth. *Family.*

The Power of Reflection

For many years, reflecting was something I didn't think I had time for. Teaching a lab-based class where time was limited and daily cleanup was essential meant that reflection time fell by the wayside. I knew it was important and felt guilty about it, but for too many years, it just didn't happen; then, a few years ago, I decided to make reflection a priority regardless of the challenging time constraints. This was one of the best decisions I've made as a teacher. Students connect at a deeper level to what they are learning when they immediately reflect on and process their successes and failures and think through what they could improve. The valuable insight I gain into students' understanding and depth of knowledge during group and one-on-one reflections allows me to adapt my teaching to meet each student's need. It took some shifts in my practice to make time for reflecting, but it has been worth the effort.

In my class, and probably in yours too, students learn new skills and methods on a daily basis. This newly gained knowledge is often applied in culinary lab activities during which students create something. After completing the lab, each team brings me their dish for evaluation—a strategy I added to build in a time for immediate reflection. We taste the dish together and discuss the flavor, texture, and appearance. Students reflect on what went right, wrong, and what they would do differently next time. This reflection time would lose its power if I were to wait till the next day. It's important that it happens in real time while the learning experience is fresh in their minds. It doesn't have to take a long time, but thinking through their learning is a very important part of their lab experience. I also find that students take their lab more seriously when they know they will be bringing it to me for evaluation. To motivate them even more, I give product quality badges to the teams that score the highest. Bringing in competition further elevates their level of engagement as well as their desire to do their very best.

My students—and probably yours too—crave authentic feedback and are disappointed on days that time doesn't allow it. Do I always feel like eating eighteen bites of the same dish? Oh goodness, no! But the payoff of meaningful learning that sticks is huge.

#FOODSNAPS

Another strategy I use for reflection is #FoodSnaps, an idea I adapted from Tara Martin's (@TaraMMartinEDU) #BookSnaps found on tarammartin.com. When I first read her post on Dave Burgess' blog, I immediately adopted the idea of making learning and thinking visible by snapping pictures of what I was reading and adding bitmojis, emojis, thought bubbles, and text. As a visual learner, #BookSnaps provided me with a powerful reflection opportunity. I created my own #BookSnaps of what I was reading, made deeper connections to the text, and retained more of what I had read.

My next step was to find a way to adapt this idea for my culinary world. It can be difficult to build in time at the end of every class period for evaluation and reflection on learning, but the reality is that sometimes we run out of time. In my classroom, learning is messy—literally. With dishes to clean, counters to sanitize, and floors to sweep, the end of class can be rushed. There isn't always enough time to taste the food and give valuable feedback. This was a problem. When students make amazingly delicious food, what do they want to do? Eat it, of course! It would be cruel and unusual punishment to make them wait to eat it until the next day. I needed a solution that would allow for immediate reflection even when we ran out of time on those busy lab days.

Then I had a thought: *My students love to take pictures of their food and post them to Snapchat and Instagram. How cool would it be if they created #FoodSnaps of their finished products while their learning was still fresh in their minds and posted them to a Padlet? We could look at them the next day and evaluate together as a class!* I had a good feeling this was the answer I was looking for!

I couldn't wait to get my students foodsnappin' the next day. I created a Padlet with columns for each period and shared the link on my daily announcement in our Google Classroom. As I gave students instructions for the day's lab, I explained we were going to reflect a little differently. I mirrored my phone to our AppleTV and gave them a quick tutorial on how to upload their pictures to Padlet. Most already used Snapchat, so they immediately caught on to the idea and couldn't wait to start snappin'!

There are so many things I love about reflecting with #FoodSnaps:

Flexibility

Time is of the essence in culinary classes. Not every team finishes at the same time. One false move during the lab, and it can set a team back ten or more minutes. Some students finish their creations with time to spare, and others are running out the door in a frenzy as the bell rings. Flexible reflecting allows some students to complete their #FoodSnaps during class if there is time, and others can wait till they get home and have time to process.

Personalized Reflection

I love that, in a class where students are collaborating in teams to create, they have an opportunity to personalize their creations with bitmojis, emojis, backgrounds, and text. It also allows for them to reflect individually on their learning, making connections to past recipes they've made or food they've eaten.

Snaps Speak Their Language

As my friend Tara says, "Let's speak in a language that kids understand." Students were already speaking in "Snapchat" language and sharing their pictures of food with friends and family. Why not use this in a deeper and more meaningful way to reflect on learning?

Global Connections

One way we've taken #FoodSnaps to another level is by sharing our learning through global collaborations. Brandi Miller's first-grade class in Auburndale, Florida, has partnered with my classes to experience a little piece of culinary with us. I have shared the link to our #FoodSnaps Padlet, and her students vote on their favorite with the star feature! My students love to share their creations with these first graders, and the first graders love to take part in the learning by voting on their favorites.

Share Recipes

With the link feature in Snapchat, students can upload their recipes. Not only do they have a visual representation of their learning, they can share that learning—with resources attached. Students can also upload sketchnotes and other resources they've created as part of their reflection.

Flipgrid

Another fabulous method for student reflection is Flipgrid. Flipgrid is a video-discussion platform that allows teachers to create grids and topic boards for students to record their video responses. The tool is both robust, with lots of features to choose from, and extremely intuitive. Flipgrid is a great way for students to reflect and share what they know. I pose a question or prompt on the board and then students answer the question or prompt via video. Some of my students are self-conscious of their videos being shared, which makes the ability to keep the videos private for only me to see very handy. Flipgrid adds flexibility to my schedule too, as it allows me to play the videos after class when I can take time to comment and assess how well students are understanding the techniques, methods, and overall content being taught.

Make Time for Authentic Learning Experiences

Authentic audiences make learning experiences more meaningful. When your students are creating something exclusively for you, they'll do a good job. When they know a professional outside the classroom, their peers, or even a global audience on social media will see their work, they'll do a *great* job. Part of authentic learning is getting feedback from that authentic audience and then reflecting on what worked and what could be improved next time.

- ✳ Whom could you invite into the classroom as part of an authentic audience for your students?
- ✳ What opportunities do your students have to participate in competition outside the classroom?
- ✳ How can you use reflection to enhance your students' learning experiences?

Chapter 8

Legacy

If you could only sense how important you are to the lives of those you meet, how important you can be to the people you may never even dream of. There is something of yourself that you leave at every meeting with another person.

–Fred Rogers

One day I was sitting in the waiting room of a local beauty salon when a lady whom I recognized immediately walked in. The red hair, sparkling eyes, and infectious smile could only belong to one person: my fifth-grade teacher. Though I hadn't seen her since I graduated from elementary school, there was no mistaking her. She had made an imprint on my heart. As she walked by, I knew I couldn't leave the salon without having the opportunity to introduce myself. I had to let her know that she had made a difference in my life.

As I waited for the right moment to walk over, my mind instantly flashed back to that childhood year when I'd had a mouthful of crooked teeth and a shy and sensitive disposition. So many awkward, embarrassing moments from that year flooded over me in a matter of seconds. I remembered the time a boy pushed my head into the drinking fountain while I was taking a sip, and I started crying, and the time when I belted out singing the wrong song during choir practice, and everyone burst into laughter. If those two weren't bad enough, there was the horrific memory of taking the walk of shame back to class after a "lice check" with a note saying I was "infected." I'll never forget handing my teacher the note, terrified that she would think I was a dirty kid; instead, she looked at me with a compassionate smile and made me feel that I was perfectly normal.

Oh, there are more. Remember that fifth-grade music class experience where I was told my lips were too big for the flute? Yep, that was another traumatic experience that happened all in the same year. All this to say that this teacher with red hair and sparkling eyes accepted me and believed in me, crooked teeth and all. She made me feel normal when my sensitive soul told me I wasn't. This teacher was also the only one I ever had who gamified her classroom. I'm sure she didn't call it that, and I don't remember the details except that we were traveling across Oregon in a stagecoach, and we had a bulletin board where we tracked our journey. She made learning an adventure, and I loved it.

After a few moments of reflecting on why this teacher was so memorable, the opportunity came to approach her. With tears in my eyes and warmth in my heart, I introduced myself to her. Her eyes lit up as a look of recognition illuminated her face. I have no idea if she really remembered me or not, but her response made me realize why I adored her so as a kid. She cared about me and nurtured and protected a little heart that was so tender and fragile. Though I had so many embarrassing and hurtful memories of that year, I shared with her how much of a difference she had made in my life and how her kindness and gentleness shined far brighter in my mind. As I spoke, her eyes flooded with tears, and she gave me a huge embrace. As a teacher myself, I know how special it was to her that I had taken that moment to express my appreciation for the impact she had made on my life. We all want to feel as if we've made a difference in our students' lives.

As teachers, we have the opportunity to be that bright light in our students' days. Often times we are completely unaware of the embarrassing moments they have experienced or hurtful words that have pierced their hearts. Despite those hurts, our warm smiles and kindness can illuminate the darkest of days. With each interaction, we are making a difference and leaving a legacy. We may never know the impact we have on many of our students. Beauty salon encounters don't always happen, and there are many students I may never see again once they leave my class. Regardless, I will continue to shine my light bright because I'm going to make an impact one way or another.

Celebrate and Reflect

Ending the year in my culinary class has always brought a significant layer of stress. Instead of winding down, we amp up to prepare Senior Board refreshments for seven hundred-plus people. Senior Boards typically happen the last week of school, immediately after we head into cleanup and inventory mode to close out the year. Instead of finishing up in a fun, positive way, we often end the year with the students' least favorite activity: cleaning. This is not the last memory I want my students to have of my class. The end of the year should be filled with happiness, joy, and time to celebrate and reflect!

After so many hectic last days of school, I determined to close the year out right. Because Senior Boards are the last two days for our seniors, we don't see them again until graduation. This means that while we are frantically scurrying around in catering mode the last few days in my class, we have no time for reflection or celebration of all these seniors have accomplished. To change that, I decided I would invite my seniors back the day after Senior Boards to join our underclassmen for a time of celebration and reflection. We cooked French toast and bacon and set up our tables in a big square so we could all eat together as a family. Once everyone had settled around the tables with their breakfasts, I played a video of all the pictures taken throughout the year (I think I counted three hundred). You could hear a pin drop, and maybe a few sniffles, as students looked back at all they had accomplished and all the amazing memories they had made. Once the video was over, I announced the winner of our semester-long competition, the Amazing Food Truck Race, and talked about each team and the growth I had observed throughout the course of the semester. I also shared a few of my own favorite memories and gave the students a chance to share as well. The winning team received a personalized apron and their picture went up on our Legacy Wall. After our time of reminiscing about the food truck race, I called up each senior, handed them a tumbler filled with candy, and shared what I appreciated about each one and my favorite memories of them. I cried, my students cried, and my heart was full.

There are no words to adequately describe how powerful that time with my students was. We took time to appreciate the journey, reflect on the growth from failures and successes, recognize the strengths of each individual, and savor the memories made. Was my classroom a mess? Yes! Was it totally worth it? *Absolutely*! It was the first end-of-year celebration that has become an annual tradition that honors the legacy our students leave when they graduate.

When Students Give Back

My Culinary 4 students have an opportunity every year to compete in a state culinary competition. This is not just any competition; this is a highly competitive, extremely serious demonstration of skill, speed, and team efficiency. Signing up to compete means months of preparation to create a three-course menu and practicing it over and over again until it can be prepared in sixty minutes with no electricity and a very small work space. To adequately prepare my students for this competition, it is important to have an industry mentor to help students refine their skills and learn how to work under extreme pressure.

In the last two years, I have been very fortunate to have a former student, now a Culinary Institute of America at Greystone graduate and local pastry chef, mentor our students for competition. He was actually on our very first competition team, so to have him take time to give back to our students is extremely meaningful. He experienced the pressure, stress, and dedicated hours of practice it took to compete, which means he is able to relate in a way that many could not. Students immediately connect with him because he was in the same place they are now. They are able to see how experiences in my class have propelled him forward into a career that he loves. The possibilities of their future dreams become more attainable and real as they see firsthand a former student living them out. He is able to share stories of how he started out as a timid boy lacking confidence, and with each step out of his comfort zone tackling new challenges, he has had the opportunity to pursue his passions. That is a powerful testimony coming from someone who once stood in their same spot. His legacy is making a direct difference in the lives of students. Now, that's *magical.*

Coming Full Circle

I recently went to a new, highly-acclaimed restaurant in my area to celebrate my sister's birthday. We had enjoyed delicious appetizers and were moving on to the second course when I felt a tap on my shoulder. I turned around, and to my surprise, it was a former student who was asking me if I was enjoying the meal. Come to find out, he was the chef who had prepared our food! What a magical moment! Nothing is better than seeing former students who have taken the skills learned in your class and are using them to build a career that they are passionate about. Living in a small community, these encounters happen often, and they never lose their impact. It's a beautiful thing when a passion and career come together, and you know you played a part in the journey.

Legacy Leaver

My husband and I had just watched our high school football team play—and lose—in their first-ever football championship. We held the lead, starting with our first field goal, until the last ten seconds of the game when, with the final play, the opposing team's kicker made a three-point field goal to win the game by one point.

Just as I turned my teary gaze away from the heartbroken players on the field and began to walk down the bleachers, I saw a familiar face walking toward me. The tears started pouring as I embraced a former student. This was a kid who had been in my classes for four consecutive years. He had taken all of the culinary classes I offered; I had mentored him in his senior project and had had the honor of walking him across the stage at graduation. In fact, I remember watching him with the same tear-filled eyes at his last football game of his senior year.

Right then and there, we caught up on how his life had taken shape since he had walked across the stage six years earlier. As we said our goodbyes, I said the same thing I had told him many times before: "I believe in you. I always have."

He quickly responded, “I know; remember my Senior year when I was about to walk out and never come back? I wouldn’t have graduated if it wasn’t for you.”

All the memories came flooding back, and I said, “Oh, I remember. I’ll never forget.” I remember exactly where we were standing in my classroom when he told me he was done with school. He was a kid who had endured more disappointment and heartache than any kid should have to face. He so desperately wanted to have a functional family that loved and supported him. His dad was in prison, his mom addicted to drugs, and his sister was making her own series of poor life decisions. Over the course of his four years, I saw beyond his tough, angry exterior to a kid with a heart of gold who just wanted to be accepted and loved.

Two short months away from graduation, this 230-pound, six-foot-two-inch football player came storming into my classroom, saying he was giving up on school. He had called his grandma to pick him up, and he wasn’t coming back—ever. The obstacles that stood before him to graduate felt too great to overcome, and he planned to walk out of school forever. As I faced off with the big kid towering over me, I looked straight into his eyes, and with tears streaming down my face, I said, “I have believed in you for four years, and there is absolutely no way I am going to let you do that. Dial up your grandma right now and tell her you are staying. We are going to talk to your teachers and figure out exactly what you need to do to walk across that stage. I am announcing you at graduation, and that’s all there is to it.”

I remember very clearly the walk across campus with him lumbering behind me on our way to talk to his other teachers. Those two months were probably the most emotionally difficult I’ve experienced as a teacher, but it was worth it. He walked across the stage two months later as I announced his name to receive his diploma.

Seeing him all those years later, a dad of five kids with a steady job and dreams for his future, made my heart burst with pride. All this kid needed was someone to believe in him and have faith that he could break the cycle of addiction and poor choices that had preceded him. Though I was someone in this kid's life who believed in him, I know I was not the only one. His high school football team had also become a family. He told me how this was the first football game he had been able to sit through since he had graduated because he missed playing the game that had meant so much to him during his high school years. Many others in his life helped him through as well.

This quote by Jon Gordon, author of *The Energy Bus*, sums up the way I want my students to remember me: "The best legacy you could leave is not some building that is named after you or a piece of jewelry but rather a world that has been impacted and touched by your presence, your joy, and your positive actions." You may never know the impact you make on another's life, but you *are* leaving a legacy.

Be a Hero

Whether we're a preschooler or a young teen, a graduating college senior or a retired person, we human beings all want to know that we're acceptable, that our being alive somehow makes a difference in the lives of others.

–Fred Rogers

I love reflecting with students at the end of each semester and hearing their perspectives on all that they learned. They give the most amazing ideas, and I take their feedback and use it to refine my practice and improve the experience for the next group of students who come through my door.

Not long ago, as I was standing by my door greeting my new students, a former student stopped and asked, "Hey, did you use that idea I had about creating a new item that students can earn?" When I truthfully said, "Yes," his face immediately lit up. He said, "A teacher has never used one of my ideas before!" He was blown away. The fact of the matter was, his idea *was* amazing and one that improved the learning experience for the students who took the class the following semester and, I'm sure, many more to follow. This idea did not come from a student with a high GPA or gleaming behavioral record from his other teachers. It was generated from a student who struggled, one who continually sought negative attention and whom the campus monitors and administration knew by name.

When I thought about this, it made me realize how, as human beings, we all just want to know that we are accepted and valued; we all want to make a difference in others' lives. How can we not only be heroes in our students' lives but also help them to realize they are heroes too? What they do matters, and they can make a significant impact on the lives of others and the world around them. When we give students the opportunity to share their ideas, and we put them to action, it makes them realize their value, and they are more likely to continue to contribute their ideas in the future.

Heroes... the kind of people who help all of us come to realize that 'biggest' doesn't necessarily mean 'best,' that the most important things of life are inside things like feelings and wonder and love—and that the ultimate happiness is being able sometimes, somehow, to help our neighbor become a hero too.

—Fred Rogers

Legacy Wall

To celebrate those who have taken their learning and risk-taking to impressive levels, I have created a Legacy Wall in my classroom. Those who reach MasterChef status three times within a semester, through successful completion of quests, challenges, and missions, will be celebrated by their picture forever being displayed in our classroom. Students on the Legacy Wall have leaped beyond their comfort zone to conquer great odds. Not only is their picture displayed, but I also have an apron embroidered with their name on it that they can wear proudly as a symbol of the impact they made on their peers and our classroom. I tell students that they are leaving a legacy in our classroom that will be carried on throughout future school years as a reminder of those who have come before them. It's a big deal. Kids love that their names will be carried on at South Medford High School.

Above All, Have a Good Time

I have a sign that hangs by my classroom door that quotes Julia Child: "Above all, have a good time!" This is a reminder to me that in all the demands and initiatives we encounter in education, we need to focus on why we got into this business in the first place. I want to bring passion to the classroom every day and remember to have a good time learning along with my kids.

Passion is contagious, and if students see us passion-filled and having fun, they are going to catch that passion too. I want students to learn skills in my class that they will continue to build on for a lifetime. Twenty years from now, whether my students are working in the restaurant industry or cooking dinner for their friends and family, I want them to look back on their experience in culinary arts with fond memories and know that what they learned has made a difference in their lives. My students are not just learning culinary skills; they are also learning life skills. They are learning how to critically think, problem solve, create, empathize, collaborate, and communicate. Each of these skills is essential in life and provides students with the confidence needed to launch into pursuit of their passions.

I was riding up to a conference with a regional EdTech colleague this past year, and I began sharing a little bit about my family. My dad spent most of his years as a highly successful and respected track and cross-country coach at a community college in Southern California but had spent a year in Southern Oregon interim coaching at the university. As I began sharing about my dad with my colleague, he interrupted me mid-sentence and exclaimed, "I think I know your dad! He made a significant impact on my life and track memories." He went on to share how my dad had come at a pivotal time in his college track career. He was a state record holder with a bright future ahead of him and, due to an unfortunate set of circumstances, was ready to give up and quit the program. My dad stepped into the program at that time as a volunteer coach and gave up his early mornings and evenings to coach and give the support and guidance that my colleague desperately needed. My dad had made a huge difference in his life.

My dad has always been a hero to me, and I admire him greatly. He left such a tremendous legacy on the sport of track and cross country that he has been inducted into four halls of fame. Although looking back on my dad's career, this short time span in Southern Oregon was not one that would have stood out to him as a highlight; in fact, it was a time that was marked with discouragement. He was employed at a job that was not in his passion area and had volunteered at the university because he loved coaching so much. Yet to this young boy, his impact had been so impactful that he remembers it as a landmark time in his life. Wow! When he shared this story with me, it gave me chills.

Every day we have the power of transforming students' lives. What kind of legacy will you leave in your profession? The heartfelt letters, the hair salon, and the football game encounters we have with our students are fun and encouraging reminders of the impact we have. But they are a handful out of hundreds or even thousands of the students whose lives you touch as a teacher. When you have fun, when you live with passion and empower your students to do the same, you are leaving a legacy that will last forever.

Leave a Legacy

As educators we have a tremendous opportunity to not only leave our own legacy but to also help our students develop their skills, pique their curiosity, and discover their passions so they can be legacy leavers too.

- In what ways can you celebrate your students' success?
- How can you help your students realize they are heroes—that they can leave a positive legacy wherever they go?
- What kind of legacy will you leave?

Chapter 9

Go Make Some Magic!

Step back four years. In my Culinary Arts classroom, I had things dialed in. Lessons were running smoothly, I was comfortable, students were learning, but I was really just going through the motions. I had lost a bit of my spark; the magic was missing.

The catalyst that restored the magic was learning what it meant to be a connected educator. Connecting to other educators from around the world invigorated me and helped me rekindle the flame that had been dying. The transformation started with lurking on Twitter. I was amazed at the ideas that were being shared. I started to slowly bring new ideas to my classroom, and before long, I was tweeting what my students were learning.

Truth be told, I felt like I was a new teacher all over again at first. When I started disrupting my well-oiled machine, it was super uncomfortable. This was a huge stretch for me! There were days I wanted to throw the iPads out the window. It took time and tweaking until I found a classroom flow that worked. Slowly I added new innovations as I found ways to improve the workflow and create a classroom environment where students were immersed more deeply in learning than they had been before.

Twitter transformed the way that I looked at learning. Every time I scrolled through my feed, I was finding new things to try. I began to jump into Twitter chats and found others who were as passionate about education as I was and eager to exchange ideas and offer advice. I found these new friendships and inspiration I was encountering to be contagious. The more I connected and learned, the more I wanted to continue to connect and learn. When I shared new ideas that I had tried in my classroom, I was met with encouragement and validation from the Twittersphere that I was on track.

I've grown and changed as an educator, but when it comes down to it, my students are the ones who benefit. My connections and learning results in connections and learning for my students. When I model risk-taking, they feel safe to take risks as well.

My PLN became more than the people I collaborated with once a week on campus; they became a globally connected group of educators from whom I could continuously learn from and grow with. I was learning ideas I could immediately try, and I began sharing things that were happening in my classroom as well. I soon began to realize that more people were looking into the walls of my classroom on Twitter than they were in my own building.

I can't overstate the value of being a connected educator. I have grown exponentially and developed friendships that inspire, encourage, and uplift me on a daily basis. I am a far better educator today than I ever would have been without this amazing network of professionals who passionately love educating our youth and doing everything to create the most amazing learning experiences possible. Finding your tribe and globally connecting with educators is truly magical. Jump in and take the risk. You will be amazed at the incredible adventures on which it will take you!

Magical Learning Through My Kids' Eyes

It's nearly impossible to choose just one experience that a teacher gave me that impacted me immensely, as I can think of several. If it hadn't been for my third grade teacher and his great enthusiasm, I wouldn't have the love for reading that I do now. And if my fifth grade teacher hadn't taught our class the importance of taking care of the earth and the impact we have on our world, I would be less conscious in my travels and daily life of my effect on the environment. In middle school, a teacher showed me that I have agency in my life and can make decisions to better myself. One of my passionate high school teachers taught me the value of hard work and dedication, while another gave me an appreciation for classic works of literature and their relevance, some that I never would have read or enjoyed without their insight. Every teacher I've had has shaped me in some way, whether it be through their subtle life lessons, enthusiasm, encouragement, or passion. One of the most prominent lessons I've learned from amazing teachers has been the significance of authenticity. I think I gained the most when teachers were authentic in their knowledge, their mistakes, and their values. That authenticity helped me in becoming an individual who strives to be transparent in my goals and intentions and, ultimately, be the best version of myself. I am beyond thankful for all of the lessons that dedicated teachers have given me, likely without even knowing the impact they've had, and continue to have, in my life.

—**Ella Richmond** (age 19)

I've had a lot of good teachers, but my second grade teacher was one of my favorites. This school year especially stood out because it was the only year that I don't remember having any anxiety about school; I was always excited to go. Looking back, it is easy to identify the ways that he made me feel safe and relaxed as a student.

I'll never forget how he began the year. He played a lot of games where he would learn students' names, he shared about himself, and established a predictable routine that I could count on. By doing this from the beginning, he created an environment where students felt safe to ask questions and be themselves.

He also allowed me to be myself. Because he had taken the time to get to know us, he could tell how people were feeling based on their moods. When I was feeling down or not acting like myself, I remember him checking to see how I was doing, which made me feel like I mattered to him. As a kid that has always battled with high anxiety, he put me at ease right from the start of the day by greeting me with a secret handshake, as he did with each of his students.

We got to know Mr. G as a person. He would bring in his guitar, dog, favorite foods, and other things he was passionate about, so we could get to know him. I also remember regularly putting on our boots and going out to the nearby creek to learn about nature. Learning was exciting because instead of just talking about it, we were experiencing it. Our desks were in groups of four, so we could collaborate and get to know those students really well. It helped me feel bonded to students around me, so I felt safe asking them questions and working together on certain activities. This incorporation of group projects allowed students to work in their strength area and encouraged students to get out of their comfort zone and feel more connected to others in class.

One experience I remember clearly was how he highlighted a different student each week of the school year by making him or her the "Big Cheese." That week felt like a holiday for that student. Everyone looked forward to this week because of how special he made them feel. Three things that made this week special were how he highlighted their interests by having them do a show and tell, gave them a chance to share about their families, and made them line leader for the week. Additionally we got to choose the songs he'd play on the guitar. I specifically remember, during that week, I chose "Puff, the Magic Dragon" for him to play every day.

Reflecting on this classroom experience made me realize how much those little things that Mr. G did meant to me. His getting to know me personally and finding out what I was passionate about made me feel more connected. He also created experiences that were collaborative and authentic, so that learning became magical.

—**Tommy Richmond** (age 16)

The Magic Is in YOU!

I was a few months into writing this book when I ran across this image that was posted on Instagram by Dave and Shelley Burgess. It was one of those messages that strikes when you least expect it and stays with you for weeks to follow. I took a screenshot of the message and have referred to it many times on days when I need the reminder. It says, "Tisha, Just be you. Tell your story."

In this wild and incredibly connected world, we have the unique opportunity to learn from people across the globe 24/7. We can collaborate over a Google Hangout, engage in Twitter conversations, and join in on Voxer conversations any time we wish. We can chat with our favorite authors and those who share our same passions. With this rapid fire of inspiration coming at us around the clock, it's nearly impossible not to learn and grow as an educator. Being connected has fueled my fire for education and challenged me to not settle for the status quo but to continue innovating and create a classroom where learning is magical. It is not an exaggeration to say that my teaching has been transformed by the educators in this space. My PLN continually encourages, supports, challenges, and pushes me beyond what I ever imagined was possible.

As I was chatting with a dear friend, I shared with her the image above and how it resonated with me. She brought my attention to the little words that nearly blended into the background of the image...

SMILE. HELLO, SUNSHINE. TAKE A LEAP.

I couldn't help but think of those little nudges of encouragement my PLN has always given me when I most needed it:

Smile . . . you are amazing.

Hello, Sunshine . . . I believe in you.

Take a leap . . . you've got this.

Even in the midst of this amazing support and encouragement, I can allow those words to blend in to the background and begin to compare, to doubt, and to second-guess the value of my story; in fact, my story has been so largely impacted by so many that I sometimes start wondering how much of it is my own. Where am I in it all? As I battled those negative thoughts that were once again beginning to surface, my friend asked me this:

What's your "WHY?"

I went to bed too tired to answer but with the question on my heart. I didn't spend much time thinking about it the following day, yet when I had a moment to message her back without hesitation, I wrote this:

MY "WHY"

To share the power of creating magical learning spaces that are filled with joy and passion.

A place where . . .

play is encouraged.

curiosity and wonder fill the air.

creativity and collaboration are abundant, and enthusiasm is electric.

risk-taking is not only encouraged but applauded.

students are not only immersed but empowered.

memories are made, and passions are realized.

every student experiences joy in learning and leaves school ready to chase his or her wildest dreams.

I realized my "WHY" is the fire that burns deep within me.

It's made up of a collection of moments and experiences that have shaped me.

It's my heart.

It's my story.

It's my manifesto.

No one else has a story just like mine. Yet my story may be just what someone else needs to hear at that moment in time to inspire and encourage him or her in their own educational journey. So many people have helped transform and shape who I am as an educator; I want to give back and do that for others as well. The fire that burns within me might be the spark that ignites someone else's flame. There is magic in my story; there is magic in your story.

So ask yourself . . . What's my "WHY?"

and . . .

Just be You.

Smile.

Hello, Sunshine . . . Take a leap.

Tell your story.

The magic is in you

So . . . GO MAKE LEARNING MAGICAL!

Invite Tisha Richmond

to Bring a Little Magic to Your School or District

Tisha is an energetic and passionate speaker who engages and inspires audiences to transform their teaching and create unforgettable experiences in their own educational settings to make learning magical. She is available for a wide variety of customizable keynote presentations, professional development sessions, workshops, and consulting opportunities on a wide variety of educational topics including . . .

- Make Learning Magical: Innovative Strategies to Inspire, Immerse, and Empower
- The Magical Power of a Team
- The Magical Power of Creativity Unleashed
- The Magical Power of Global Connection
- The Magic of Stepping out of Your Comfort Zone
- Magical Authenticity: Making Community and Global Connections for Relevant Learning
- Magical Adventures in the Gamified Classroom

tisharichmond.com

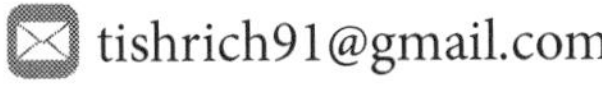
tishrich91@gmail.com

Since 2012, DBCI has been publishing books that inspire and equip educators to be their best. For more information on our DBCI titles or to purchase bulk orders for your school, district, or book study, visit **DaveBurgessConsulting.com/DBCBooks**.

More from the Like a PIRATE Series

Teach Like a PIRATE by Dave Burgess

Explore Like a Pirate by Michael Matera

Learn Like a Pirate by Paul Solarz

Play Like a Pirate by Quinn Rollins

Run Like a Pirate by Adam Welcome

Lead Like a PIRATE Series

Lead Like a PIRATE by Shelley Burgess and Beth Houf

Balance Like a Pirate by Jessica Cabeen, Jessica Johnson, and Sarah Johnson

Lead with Culture by Jay Billy

Lead with Literacy by Mandy Ellis

Leadership & School Culture

Culturize by Jimmy Casas

Escaping the School Leader's Dunk Tank by Rebecca Coda and Rick Jetter

The Innovator's Mindset by George Couros

Kids Deserve It! by Todd Nesloney and Adam Welcome

Let Them Speak by Rebecca Coda and Rick Jetter

The Limitless School by Abe Hege and Adam Dovico

The Pepper Effect by Sean Gaillard

The Principled Principal by Jeffrey Zoul and Anthony McConnell

The Secret Solution by Todd Whitaker, Sam Miller, and Ryan Donlan

Start. Right. Now. by Todd Whitaker, Jeffrey Zoul, and Jimmy Casas

Unmapped Potential by Julie Hasson and Missy Lennard

Your School Rocks by Ryan McLane and Eric Lowe

Technology & Tools

50 Things You Can Do with Google Classroom by Alice Keeler and Libbi Miller

50 Things to Go Further with Google Classroom by Alice Keeler and Libbi Miller

140 Twitter Tips for Educators by Brad Currie, Billy Krakower, and Scott Rocco

Code Breaker by Brian Aspinall

Google Apps for Littles by Christine Pinto and Alice Keeler

Master the Media by Julie Smith

Shake Up Learning by Kasey Bell

Social LEADia by Jennifer Casa-Todd

Teaching Math with Google Apps by Alice Keeler and Diana Herrington

Teaching Methods & Materials

All 4s and 5s by Andrew Sharos

Ditch That Homework by Matt Miller and Alice Keeler

Ditch That Textbook by Matt Miller

The EduProtocol Field Guide by Marlena Hebern and Jon Corippo

Instant Relevance by Denis Sheeran

LAUNCH by John Spencer and A.J. Juliani

Pure Genius by Don Wettrick

Shift This! by Joy Kirr

Spark Learning by Ramsey Musallam

Sparks in the Dark by Travis Crowder and Todd Nesloney

Table Talk Math by John Stevens

The Classroom Chef by John Stevens and Matt Vaudrey

The Wild Card by Hope and Wade King

The Writing on the Classroom Wall by Steve Wyborney

Inspiration, Professional Growth, & Personal Development

4 O'Clock Faculty by Rich Czyz

Be REAL by Tara Martin

Be the One for Kids by Ryan Sheehy

The EduNinja Mindset by Jennifer Burdis

How Much Water Do We Have? by Pete and Kris Nunweiler

P Is for Pirate by Dave and Shelley Burgess

The Path to Serendipity by Allyson Aspey

Shattering the Perfect Teacher Myth by Aaron Hogan

Stories from Webb by Todd Nesloney

Talk to Me by Kim Bearden

The Zen Teacher by Dan Tricarico

Children's Books

Dolphins in Trees by Aaron Polansky

About the Author

Tisha Richmond is a passionate and innovative district tech instructional specialist and former high school culinary arts teacher of twenty-two years from Southern Oregon. She is passionate about infusing joy, passion, play, and gamified experiences into classrooms to make learning MAGICAL. She received the 2018 Golden Pear High School Teacher of the Year award in her district and was a 2018 first-place winner in Henry Ford's Innovation Nation Teacher Innovator Awards. She is a connected educator who is continually collaborating, sharing, and learning with her personal learning network. Tisha loves sharing her passion for teaching and learning and speaks nationally on gamification and various innovative strategies.

TishaRichmond.com